HACKING ENGAGEMENT

HACKING ENGAGEMENT

50

Tips & Tools

To Engage Teachers and Learners Daily

James Alan Sturtevant

PUBLICATIONS

Hacking Engagement
50 Tips & Tools To Engage Teachers and Learners Daily

James Sturtevant

Hacking Engagement
© 2016 by Times 10 Publications

These books are available at special discounts when purchased in quantity for use as premiums, promotions, fundraising, and educational use. For inquiries and details, contact us at www.hacklearning.org.

Published by Times 10
Cleveland, OH
HackLearning.org
Cover Design by Tracey Henterly
Interior Design by Steven Plummer
Editing by Ruth Arseneault
Proofreading by Jennifer Jas
Library of Congress Control Number: 2016950711
ISBN: 978-0-9861049-6-1
First Printing: October, 2016

CONTENTS

PUBLISHER'S FOREWORD

WHAT I REMEMBER most about the wonderful teacher who taught me how to teach nearly 30 years ago are the three words she repeated daily: "Structure, structure, structure." She helped me in many ways, and for a very long time I thought her structure mantra was the perfect recipe for successful educators. Boy, was I wrong.

While a certain amount of structure can work in some classrooms, what most teachers need is some messiness—the kind of chaos that excites today's learners. It's challenging to engage students in a room driven by structure, structure, and more structure. If you have doubts, they'll disappear the moment you dive into this book and explore the many resources that engagement expert James Sturtevant shares in what promises to be the most fun you've had in recent memory while reading an education book.

In Hacking Engagement, the seventh book in the Hack Learning Series, Sturtevant smashes the original Hack Learning Series model of five or even 10 hacks, doling out 50 fantastic right-now solutions for any engagement problem you might encounter. Need tips and tools to liven up your classroom? Want to reimagine your out-of-school assignments? Are you considering giving your students more autonomy or maybe injecting a little levity into your instruction? This book is your guide.

HACKING THE HACK LEARNING FORMULA

If you've read other books in the Hack Learning Series, you know the secret sauce is the revolutionary Hack Learning Formula that is changing how we solve problems in education. While it maintains everyone's favorite section—What You Can Do Tomorrow—Hacking Engagement is a bit different from other HLS books. Because there are 50 hacks, author James Sturtevant and our amazing production team have integrated other facets of Hack Learning, like the Hack in Action, into other parts of these uniquely structured chapters. We believe you'll love this spin on the Hack Learning formula, but if you long for more detail about the brief Tips and Tools in this book, look for James Sturtevant's online Engagement course, hosted on our partner site, blendeducation.org.

I am proud to be the publisher of the Hack Learning Series and creator of the revolutionary Hack Learning Formula, which is changing how we view and solve problems daily. When you finish reading this book, you will understand how to engage even the most reluctant learner. You may begin to see solutions to other problems that you've previously overlooked. In the end, you might even become an education hacker.

And that's a good thing.

—*MARK BARNES, EDUCATION HACKER AND ENGAGER*

INTRODUCTION

FLASHBACK TO COLLEGE

I LEARNED A POWERFUL lesson about engagement in September of 1980. I was embarking on my sophomore year at Muskingum, a beautiful little liberal arts college in Southeastern Ohio. Attending a liberal arts school meant I had to take a well-rounded and diverse slate of classes. I'm a humanities guy, but I still had to take math and science—requirements that truly dogged me. On a warm and muggy late summer morning, I strolled into geology. I had selected a course friends referred to as "Rocks for Jocks" because I'd been told it was, by far, the easiest class in the hard sciences. I plopped down into a seat and waited, thinking, *This class has the potential to bore the hell out of me and implode my GPA.*

What happened next was transformational. In traipsed a diminutive professor. He wore a flannel shirt and old khakis. Out of his face erupted a tremendous black beard that ended below his collar bones. He was relaxed and informal, but he seemed a bit persnickety. As he launched into his initial monologue, it became clear that he had a droll sense of humor. He described the problems inherent in being a married geologist: "You see, to me, a billion years is a blink of an eye. So it's very tough for me to get excited about being fifteen minutes late to meet my wife."

I was so relieved that I was going to be taught by a scientist with a personality, a scientist with spunk and humor. Over the next month, I grew to love going to geology. The class was fun; the prof was hilarious. I ended up earning a B.

In my geology class, I bonded with the professor. Our relationship altered my experience of the class so that instead of being so bored and disengaged that I failed to learn, I chose to participate and absorb the content. This story may have a familiar ring. Many people have been reluctant learners who ended up liking a class they feared because of a cool, engaging teacher.

Hacking Engagement: 50 Tips and Tools to Engage Teachers and Learners Daily will be your roadmap to create an engaging class that your learners, even the reluctant ones, will love. Rest assured, this book contains a bevy of relationship directives, but that's not all. It also includes awesome tech tools and innovative strategies to make your class irresistible.

Each of the fifty hacks begins with a thorough explanation of a problem that teachers commonly face. Then I offer a detailed solution that anyone can easily use to engage students. I'll finish up by giving you concrete steps to implement the solution the next day.

I want to assure you that I'm one of you. I'm not an administrator. I'm not a consultant. I'm not a professor. I'm a teacher, and I'm in the trenches with you. My mission is to figure out how I can engage my students in my public school classroom. It's a mission I've been on for over three decades.

When I was in the process of crafting this book, I launched the *Hacking Engagement* podcast, which mirrors and supplements these pages. As you read,

Image 0.1: Podcast Episode: Hello Colleague

you'll frequently encounter QR codes that will connect you to episodes. If you're new to QR codes, no worries. Hack 1 will show you exactly how to use them. These codes will enable you to hear my voice and the voices of some fascinating contributors to *Hacking Engagement*. Some QR codes will direct you to other bonus content that will help you become an engagement expert. Now, point your QR code app to Image 0.1 and you'll be whisked away to a virtual space where you can hear more about my quest to help you bond with your students tomorrow.

You're on your way to hacking engagement in your own classroom. Begin with these fifty powerful tips and tools, any of which you can use tomorrow.

HACK 1

ENTICE RELUCTANT READERS WITH QR CODES

THE PROBLEM: MANY STUDENTS ARE RELUCTANT READERS

READING FOR SCHOOL was a painful reality for me as a fourth grader. I resisted reading assignments that some stuffy adult teacher thought would benefit me. It was like being told, "Eat your vegetables." However, when I was at home and free to make my own selections, I did enjoy reading. I used to devour *MAD Magazine*. It was funny, it had compelling and creative artwork, it expanded my vocabulary, and it taught me about current events. My parents, much to their credit, fully endorsed my proclivity to read *MAD*.

The challenge for teachers who have reluctant readers is to engage them. If you can genuinely pique their interest, they'll read voluntarily. Perhaps you could draw on the same things that attracted me to *MAD* to entice students with your reading assignments. Jennifer Wilson's exciting book trailers do just that.

I call Jennifer Wilson "The Quick Response Woman." In her position as a school district's coordinator of instruction and innovation, one of her main tasks is to help teachers with technology. She's amazingly responsive, but that's not why she's "The Quick Response Woman": Jennifer is all about the Quick Response (QR) code. The QR code is more than just an innocent-looking square filled with interesting symbols. It's an amazing doorway that links a person directly to virtual content.

Jennifer became fascinated with how a teacher could use QR codes to build excitement about reading. She uses them to link students to alluring information about books in the form of book trailers. Just as a successful movie trailer engages the audience to the point where they become obsessed with watching the show, book trailers draw in potential readers. She says:

> During Read Across America week, I observed elementary students create movie trailers for their favorite books. Students then generated a QR code and taped it on the back of their specific book in the library, so other students who haven't read the book could get a sneak peek of the book's plot. Other students used Aurasma, a free augmented-reality app, to make the book title come to life. How it worked was when a student opened the app on a device and held it over the title of the book, the movie trailer would begin to play, making the book turn into a movie.

THE HACK: TEACH STUDENTS TO CREATE QR CODE TRAILERS TO HOOK THE NEXT READER

This hack can work for required or self-selected reading. Much like your standard movie trailers, the book trailer should build anticipation that engages the potential audience. This video trailer could be a dramatization in the form of a student-produced video, or a Google Slides or Moovly presentation that has been uploaded to YouTube. Students will then create a QR code to guide classmates to their masterpiece. Finally, they'll print the QR code and physically attach it to the book or reading handout. Classmates will circulate around the room, scan various codes, and then evaluate each trailer.

You might consider creating your own classroom version of the Academy Awards. Students could nominate trailers based on such categories as best acting, strongest visual appeal, and best screenplay. Ultimately, your class will award "The Trailer of the Year" to the video that most inspired them to dive into the reading.

Image 1.1: Talking QR Codes

If you're unfamiliar with QR codes, download a QR code reader from your app store (just type "QR" into the search field and plenty of free options will appear). Then scan Image 1.1 and you'll be whisked away to some powerful information about using QR codes, which you can share with students when teaching them how to create QR codes for their movie trailers.

WHAT YOU CAN DO TOMORROW

- **Select a book or reading selection.** Your objective is for students to build an unquenchable thirst for this reading. Make certain the reading material you select lives up to the awesome trailers kids will produce.

- **Learn about QR codes and how to use them.** Research QR codes online or talk to a friend or colleague, or maybe a tech savvy student, about the best apps and how to create and read QR codes. Remember to download a free QR code reader from your app store.

- **Produce a QR code for the lesson prompt.** This could be a quick link to your Google Classroom or teacher website. Reproduce the QR code and attach it to various desktops, the door, a window, the floor, obscure sections of your wall, and perhaps even on a willing student's book bag. Instruct students to find all the codes (which they'll have fun doing) and then scan and react. This will be a hands-on demonstration of how to use QR codes for them and for you. (Remember, we're better together than we are apart.)

- **Create the student prompt for the trailers.** The specifics for this assignment are entirely up to you. Ask yourself these questions to guide your movie trailer instructions: How do you want the trailers to look? How long should they be? What elements (people, props, scenery, etc.) should be included?

- **Develop categories for the Academy Awards presentation.** Decide what production and content aspects you want to evaluate and celebrate.

Many students are reluctant readers who need to be enticed to delve into books. A great way to do this is to attach a QR code to an assigned reading. It'll act as a doorway to student engagement. Readers who click on the code will be catapulted into a movie that promotes the book they hold in their hands.

HACK 2

ADVENTURES IN CLASSROOM MANAGEMENT

THE PROBLEM: YOUR CLASS MAKES YOU QUESTION EDUCATION AS A CAREER CHOICE

IF YOU MET Andy Jados on a plane, or at a party, or on vacation, you'd probably be shocked to learn he's a high school principal. He just doesn't seem like one. He's so funny and nice. Interacting with him is a pleasure. As a principal, Andy reassures, empowers, and engages struggling teachers by embracing his own early challenges. His first principal gig was in a tough urban district. In such a setting, being friendly and nice and making people smile would not seem like essential attributes. But Andy's school thrived under his leadership. He's learned that putting the effort into organizing a congenial atmosphere benefits everyone.

Ironically, Andy's biggest student engagement challenge occurred, not in a stereotypically difficult urban school but at an affluent suburban school when he was a young teacher.

He had some seriously disengaged students. Andy became an outstanding educator thanks in part to this transformational experience early in his career. Here's how Andy described his predicament: "The last period of the day, I had a class of only thirteen students, but I was continually frustrated. I could not keep them on task." Andy had a class that was chaotic and disengaged. It was a class late in the day and his students had already mentally checked out.

THE HACK: MANAGE YOUR CLASS WITH ORGANIZED ROUTINES

Andy was frustrated, but he's a man of action. He responded to his predicament by playing to his strength—organization. He discovered the prime distractions in his class and made a plan to eliminate them. While some of the strategies he employed appear quite simple, perhaps even obvious, the key to success is in the pacing. Andy's story is the perfect example of this hack.

I finally decided to change every classroom routine. I had new procedures for everything. If I had papers to hand out, I would give them to one student and that person would start the process of making sure each row had what it needed. When students entered and exited the classroom, they would sign in or out on a clipboard. There would be a question put on the board, which they knew to answer in their journals. While they wrote, I would take attendance and check homework. There was absolutely no downtime during the lesson. I actually accomplished more in that class than my others because of how efficiently it ran. As an administrator, I have always made sure to remember that experience. It helps me understand how frustrating it can be to teach if you do not have a classroom management procedure in place. I have used that experience multiple times to assist teachers in that area.

WHAT YOU CAN DO TOMORROW

- **Make a list of common distractions in your class.** This could include things like downtime after students have completed an activity, tardiness, students disrupting a lesson to ask for makeup work, students interrupting one another, and students asking to go to the bathroom.

- **Create an organization plan.** Generate routines to waylay distractions before they occur. Review examples of how Andy transformed his class. Apply some of his solutions, or come up with your own. Start implementing them tomorrow.

- **Promote your plan.** Explain what you're attempting and why you're attempting it. Otherwise, kids might be wondering, *Where'd this come* *from?* Let students in on your goals and you have a better chance at gaining cooperation and perhaps buy-in.

- **Assign students tasks.** Certain jobs like passing out papers, collecting papers, informing returning students of makeup work, orienting your Smart Board, distributing Chromebooks, and even taking attendance distract you from engaging kids. Deputize student helpers. You may wish to give some of your most disruptive students responsibilities. This could work wonders for engagement in your classroom.

- **Debrief students.** Empower kids to offer advice on how to improve your plan. Ask them how they would like to be deputized and what responsibilities they value. Consider using a survey tool like Twitter's poll feature or SurveyMonkey (more on this in Hack 4).

A great principal once told me that the best classroom management tools were a thorough organized lesson plan coupled with consistent classroom procedures. He was right, and the example of Andy Jados, the Organization Man, will help you get there.

LET ME SEE YOU GOOGLE

THE PROBLEM: SOME TEACHERS AND STUDENTS ARE UNFAMILIAR WITH GOOGLE

THIS BOOK WILL make frequent references to Google Classroom, Google Docs, and Google Forms. If you teach at a Google School, these references will be familiar. If you don't, becoming a Google School is easy and free.

Ed Kitchen is a school technology specialist. He's presented all over the country about how to use Google in the classroom. Here's what Ed says about becoming a Google School:

> A school that embraces Google embraces collaboration. It gives students and teachers anywhere/anytime access to all classroom documents. I once watched a class of fourth graders work with Google Docs for the first time. They were certainly engaged in the creation process, which is awesome. Later I learned that these same kids were collaborating even after school hours by using the comment features in Google Docs to interact with one another.

I was recently presented with a student teacher who was unfamiliar with Google Classroom. Within a week, he was a card-carrying Google Classroom evangelist. However, being a student teacher meant that he didn't have a school Google email account. No worries: He made his own separate school Gmail account in less than thirty seconds. The students found it effortless to interact with him electronically. This got me thinking: *Wow Google is engaging, powerful, familiar, and pervasive.*

Even a teacher at a non-Google school could harness many of the incredible advantages of this institution of the modern age. Quite simply, students are extremely comfortable expressing themselves through Google.

THE HACK: EMPOWER STUDENTS TO EXPRESS THEMSELVES WITH GOOGLE

Your first step will be to assess student understanding of Google. Log in to your school Google account. If, like my student teacher, you don't have one, create your own. Construct a Google Form comprised of two questions that measure student familiarity with Google. For example, you provide a list of Google tools, like Gmail, Google Slides, and Google Docs and ask students to check which ones they've used. Then you can ask for the Gmail address and/or provide a link where they can get one. By submitting this electronic form, students will provide you with plenty of information about their comfort levels with Google. This will allow you to support them as they move through the rest of the hack.

When students submit writing assignments, have them do it via Google Docs.

Image 3.1

Google Docs looks and feels similar to Microsoft Word. In fact, you can easily transform a Word document into a Google Doc. You go through the same steps to create a Google Doc as you did to make a Google Form. Google Docs gives teachers and students remarkable collaboration opportunities.

Challenge students to create a Google Slides presentation. Google Slides are similar to PowerPoint. Students rapidly gain confidence and mastery of this platform. Image 3.1 takes you to a *Hacking Engagement* podcast episode, in which I share more about the benefits of Google in your classroom.

WHAT YOU CAN DO TOMORROW

- **Create a Google account.** This step is only necessary if you don't teach at a Google School. If you haven't done this already, it takes less than a minute.

- **Direct learners to complete the "Google Intro" form.** You could provide the direct link via Google Classroom, provide the URL, or pass out a QR code that transports them to the page (QR codes can be useful in so many ways). When they've completed the form, direct them to submit it.

- **Share a Google Doc.** This activity might be something like a brief greeting. Instruct students to write something about themselves and share it with you, a group, or the entire class. This exercise will be foundational to future collaboration.

- **Instruct students to construct a Google Slides presentation.** This presentation will be comprised of three slides:

  1. *Interesting personal information*

  2. *Thoughts about Google's role in the classroom*

  3. *Their favorite way to express themselves with Google*
     After they've finished building their presentations, they should share them with you.

- **Create presentation groups.** Organize kids into groups of four and have them present their Google Slides to one another. This will be an engaging hands-on demonstration of the potential of this amazing tool.

The world collaborates with Google. Make certain that you interact with students via this foundational platform.

HACK 4

ENGAGE AS YOU GAUGE WITH SURVEYMONKEY

THE PROBLEM: TEACHERS DON'T KNOW STUDENT PREFERENCES

TRYING TO DETERMINE what someone else is thinking is one of life's great challenges. You may have spent the majority of a first date wondering just what was going on behind an unreadable face. Political candidates, advertisers, social scientists, product developers, and tech marketers place tremendous emphasis on gauging public sentiment. Understanding another's preferences can save time, effort, and money. When it comes to our students, let's become detective-like and solve the mysteries of their preferences. Once we know what appeals to the kids we teach, we can take advantage of this knowledge to engage them in learning.

I'm always amazed (and a little unnerved) when I'm on Facebook and I'm drawn to a compelling Amazon advertisement in the upper right-hand corner of the page. This image unfailingly promotes a product that Amazon has determined will appeal to me—it's targeted to my individual inclinations to make me feel I cannot do without it.

This digital survey tool is attractive and easy to use. It's also a lot of fun, which in itself is engaging.

Sometimes, I take the bait. It's hard to resist when the ad has been tailored to push my buttons. The worlds of business and politics have long understood the motivational power of targeting a person's preferences. Successful presidential campaigns know exactly which voters, in which crucial districts, have to be contacted and then motivated to vote. Wouldn't it be cool if teachers could take their students' preference pulse? Learning kids' buttons, like Amazon diagnosed mine, has epic engagement potential.

THE HACK: GAUGE STUDENT INTERESTS WITH A POLL

One outstanding way to poll your students is through SurveyMonkey (surveymonkey. com). This digital survey tool is attractive and easy to use. It's also a lot of fun, which in itself is engaging. You simply create the poll and then give your students the link. I post mine on Google Classroom. Student responses in SurveyMonkey are anonymous. Hence, peer pressure is mitigated. When kids don't fear ridicule, they participate and express accurately.

HERE ARE THREE WAYS TO USE SURVEYMONKEY:

- Use polls to build relationships. You could ask students to rate their favorite food or music genres. Prompt them to help you with a tough purchasing decision: "Should I buy this, or this?" Or perhaps, they can help you choose between four potential vacation destinations. Surveys, like the one in Image 4.1, make for interesting brief detours from ultra-serious academics.

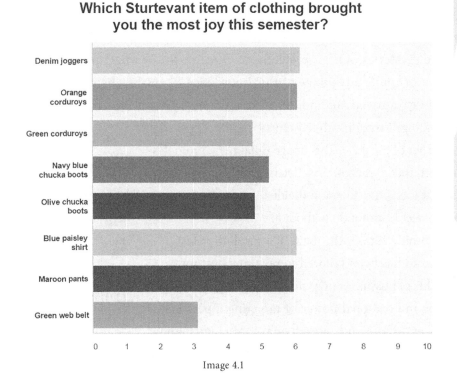

Image 4.1

- Commission students to be your engagement coaches. Ask kids to rank class activities from most to least desirable. You'll learn what they like and what they don't. Build more of their preferred activities into your repertoire and develop new ones based on the trends you notice. The more kids enjoy your class, the more engaged they'll be.

Image 4.2

- Use SurveyMonkey to captivate students in the first five minutes of class. Preview a lesson with a dilemma-type multiple-choice question. Confront students with a number of controversial quotations and force them to advocate for one.

- Conduct a weekly presidential preference poll. Students then analyze trends.

Listen to the episode of the *Hacking Engagement* podcast in Image 4.2 to learn more about engaging with SurveyMonkey.

WHAT YOU CAN DO TOMORROW

- **Sign up for SurveyMonkey.** I've conducted all my surveys with the free version.
- **Create a poll.** Try a multiple-choice or ranking question.
- **Insert a hook.** At the beginning of a lesson, challenge students to take a stand, make a prediction, or provoke them with a deep question.

If you understand student preferences, you can create a more engaging class. SurveyMonkey will help in this endeavor.

HACK 5

CREATE CELEBRITY COUPLE NICKNAMES

THE PROBLEM: TEACHERS HAVE A HARD TIME REMEMBERING STUDENTS' NAMES

WHEN I WAS in college, I endured a miserable date. I had a big crush on a girl on campus. I knew she had a boyfriend, but I thought I'd make a superior romantic partner. When I learned they'd broken up, I sprang into action. Unfortunately, on our date she called me by her ex-boyfriend's first name three times. I felt miserable. *Does she even know my name? Why am I not making an impression? Is she obsessed with her ex?* There was not a second date.

When teachers don't know student names, it can be just as catastrophic:

- I'm insignificant.

- Mr. S doesn't notice me.

- I'm not important.

- Mr. S doesn't like me.

- I'm invisible.

- Mr. S knows other students' names. He must like them better.

If you want your students engaged, you simply have to know their names. It's essential. Here's the bad news: Learning student names is a huge challenge. Not only do some educators struggle remembering names, but they have many names to remember.

> **Creating unique monikers will help you remember names. It also creates loyalty.**

I interact with 150 students daily. It's also important to master the name recall process promptly. Ten days into class, you don't want to be saying, "Hey, you in the brown shirt, what's the answer to number ten?" Engagement will not materialize if students feel marginalized. And students *will* feel marginalized if teachers don't know their names.

THE HACK: CREATE NICKNAMES FOR YOUR STUDENTS

Brad Pitt plus Angelina Jolie equals Brangelina is a solid example of a celebrity couple nickname. Morphing two names into one can be done with most students' first and last names:

- Merri Buckles becomes Merckles.

- Christopher Ward becomes Wardopher.

Sometimes you can take elements of each name, mainly hard consonant sounds, and then combine them to create familiar and expressive words:

- Samantha Bickley becomes Smack.

- Josey Burdge becomes the Surge.

And finally, some names transform into something truly creative:

- Trevor Ambrose becomes Trambrosia.

- Alexandrina Hernandez becomes Alehendrines.

Creating unique monikers will help you remember names. It'll also create loyalty to your class: *Mr. S calls me Trambrosia. That's cool.* And student loyalty equals engagement.

WHAT YOU CAN DO TOMORROW

- **Take your seating chart and create celebrity nicknames out of the first and last names.** Just the creation of the nickname itself will significantly help you in the name recall process.

- **Challenge kids to morph your name.** My favorite kid concoction was James Sturtevant equals The Vant Jam.

- **Deputize your students to create their own celebrity nicknames.** A few students may decline and that's perfectly their right. My experience has been that students really enjoy this challenge.

- **Make it a game.** Flash some images of celebrity couples up on your Smart Board and challenge students to guess their couple nickname. Alternatively, you can put the names on a social channel like Twitter, Snapchat, or Pinterest, or a digital pin board like Wordle or Note.ly. You could even have kids put their names on posters or butcher paper. No matter how you do it, kids will love it, and you'll learn their names in no time.

You can't engage kids if you don't know their names. Creating celebrity nicknames will transform this tedious chore into a fun game that students will love, and it will help you connect with them immediately.

HACK 6

CLASS PROCEDURES NIGHT AT THE IMPROV

THE PROBLEM: CLASSROOM RULES PRESENTATIONS TORMENT STUDENTS ON THE FIRST DAY OF SCHOOL

TEACHERS NEED TO think of the first day of school like opening night. What's true for Broadway and Hollywood is also true in the classroom: Opening night can make you or break you. If audiences and critics are not engaged, a show will have a short life. If students aren't engaged on day one, everyone could be in for a long semester.

Some educators approach opening classes as a time to lay down the law. They drone about the rules, the consequences, the expectations. They may be the same educators who buy into the ridiculous old adage, "Don't let them see you smile 'til Thanksgiving." *Really*? If you don't smile much before Thanksgiving, you're probably not going to smile much after.

Paranoia about anarchy is not a reason to ignore the massive engagement potential of the first classes. If you're able to grab them by the virtual lapels on day one, you'll generate significant enthusiasm for your class. Expectations must be communicated, but make certain to warmly embrace engagement too.

THE HACK: CREATE A CLASS PROCEDURES NIGHT AT THE IMPROV

Teachers often think in terms of rules. Rules tend to be punitive. How about replacing "rules" with "procedures"? Rather than setting rigid regulations that students must adhere to or risk being disciplined, procedures offer concrete actions that can easily be followed. Framing student behavior in these terms feels more positive and empowering. Once teachers embrace procedures, they need to communicate them in a more engaging way than presenting students with a list on a sheet of paper or bullets on PowerPoint slides.

Follow the improv recipe described below and make day one a blast. You'll empower kids to come up with remarkable improvs. They'll frequently create hilarious scenarios with slacker rule breakers and stern authority figures. Sure, there'll be some pushback on some of your procedures, but you should embrace the dialogue. Perhaps if you're struggling to defend a policy, you may want to rethink it. When it comes to your policies, the combination of performing an improv and participating

Image 6.1

in a debriefing discussion may lead to more student buy-in. Regardless, *Class Procedures Night at the Improv* will be an engaging, active, hilarious first day experience for your students. Expect lots of opening night five-star reviews.

If you're thinking this sounds amazing, listen to the episode of the *Hacking Engagement* podcast devoted to student improvs, linked in Image 6.1.

WHAT YOU CAN DO TOMORROW

- **Identify class procedures that would be suitable to improv.** You can then provide student groups a brief prompt like, "Demonstrate the importance of arriving on time."

- **Demonstrate an improv.** This could be a YouTube video, or perhaps you could pull aside some dramatic students before class and ask them to show how it's done.

- **Organize your student groups.** Do this before class. Allocate your dramatic kids to various groups. You want at least one ham in each acting troupe. Also distribute diligent students. It's nice for a play to have a director.

- **Give them two jobs.** They must depict the procedure and explain why it's important.

- **Display a large stopwatch or timer.** Give them one minute to come up with their improv. The large ticking numbers will add urgency and focus.

- **Prepare a class procedures handout.** This will be distributed after the improvs. It'll reinforce the performances and hopefully lead to some engaging class discussion. You'll be afforded the chance to defend policies, while at the same time, offer students a chance to be heard.

Students are often struck comatose by long, boring, repetitive rules presentations on the first day of school. The *Class Procedures Night at the Improv* will communicate important information in a highly engaging way.

HACK 7

CREATE A MOVIE TRAILER FOR YOUR CLASS

THE PROBLEM: YOU NEED A NEW WAY TO GENERATE CURIOSITY AND ENTHUSIASM FOR YOUR CLASS

EVERY YEAR YOU do the same things on the first day. You hand out a syllabus and go over the class rules. Students probably have remarkably similar experiences in their other classes. By seventh period on the first day of school, many overly indoctrinated students are ready for Christmas break. How about trying something new?

On your last movie date with your significant other, the theater probably ran some previews prior to the main feature. Your significant other probably remarked, "I can't wait to see that when it comes out." People are supremely engaged by trailers—that's the purpose of having a trailer to begin with. Try applying the same marketing tactics to your classroom.

THE HACK: CREATE A MOVIE TRAILER FOR YOUR CLASS

Instead of being part of the predictable teacher herd on day one, craft an engaging trailer for your class. Yes, this trailer can include classroom procedures, but the main focus should be on building curiosity and enthusiasm. An additional wonderful benefit of the class movie trailer is that it can be easily shown to parents. Forcing busy parents to watch your class trailer may indeed be a bridge too far, but how about if you could entice Mom or Dad to watch? Maybe you could send a promotional email, or enlist your students' help. The goal is to generate significant parent engagement and

Image 7.1

enthusiasm for what you're doing with their tender offspring. Just make sure your class movie trailer is a good one. Image 7.1 transports you to my twelve-minute class trailer.

WHAT YOU CAN DO TOMORROW

- **Create a class movie trailer.** You can screen record a PowerPoint or a Prezi and do a voice-over. I created mine on the Moovly platform. On both Moovly and Prezi, you can insert sound files. Once you've blended your voice with the presentation, upload the video file to YouTube. Then, anyone can access your trailer.

- **Create a leave-behind.** This handout would include relevant class information. But instead of you droning on about the obvious, students can simply read it for themselves.

- **Don't set the pace.** Kids watch videos constantly on their devices. Instead of showing the trailer to the entire class on the Smart Board, give students the link to the trailer and free them to watch it at their own convenience.

- **Create a buzz.** Promote your trailer on social media such as your Twitter and Facebook accounts and also your teacher website.

- **Concoct a method to entice parents to watch your trailer.** You can encourage them through an email, or perhaps you could offer students extra credit if they persuaded the parental unit to watch.

A great way to engage students and parents is to create a class movie trailer. Such a trailer affords a wonderful opportunity to build curiosity and enthusiasm for your class.

HACK 8

BUILD A STUDENT AVATAR

THE PROBLEM: TEACHERS DON'T KNOW THEIR STUDENTS

Picture this: You're driving on a Sunday afternoon, not thinking about school at all, and then suddenly, tomorrow's lesson plan forcefully presents itself. That's what happened to me last week. I was listening to a podcast about, of all things, creating a podcast. The host, John Lee Dumas, passionately promoted the idea that podcasters need to know their audience avatar. That got my attention.

Avatar is an engaging word. As soon as he said it, I immediately conjured up images of animated blue people, of Hindu gods and goddesses, of profile picture caricatures. John Lee Dumas challenges podcasters to create an avatar based on their typical listener. This creation then pilots the boat. All decisions are based on the needs of this imaginary, but very important, concoction. After listening to this segment, I knew exactly what I was going to do the next day: Build a student avatar.

THE HACK: CREATE AN AVATAR OF YOUR TYPICAL STUDENT

I teach high school students. By the time they get to me, they've completed plenty of *Tell Me About You* surveys. I wanted this information too, but I wanted to procure it in a more engaging, attractive, interactive, and enjoyable way. Such knowledge would certainly guide me in creating engaging lessons. I also wanted students to be inspired. Perhaps, they could take the information from my survey and apply it in some cool ways. Maybe they would be motivated to create their own surveys and avatars. I crafted mine (Image 8.1) on SurveyMonkey. It consisted of ten questions with drop-down menus. Half of the prompts were about demographics, the rest were about preferences.

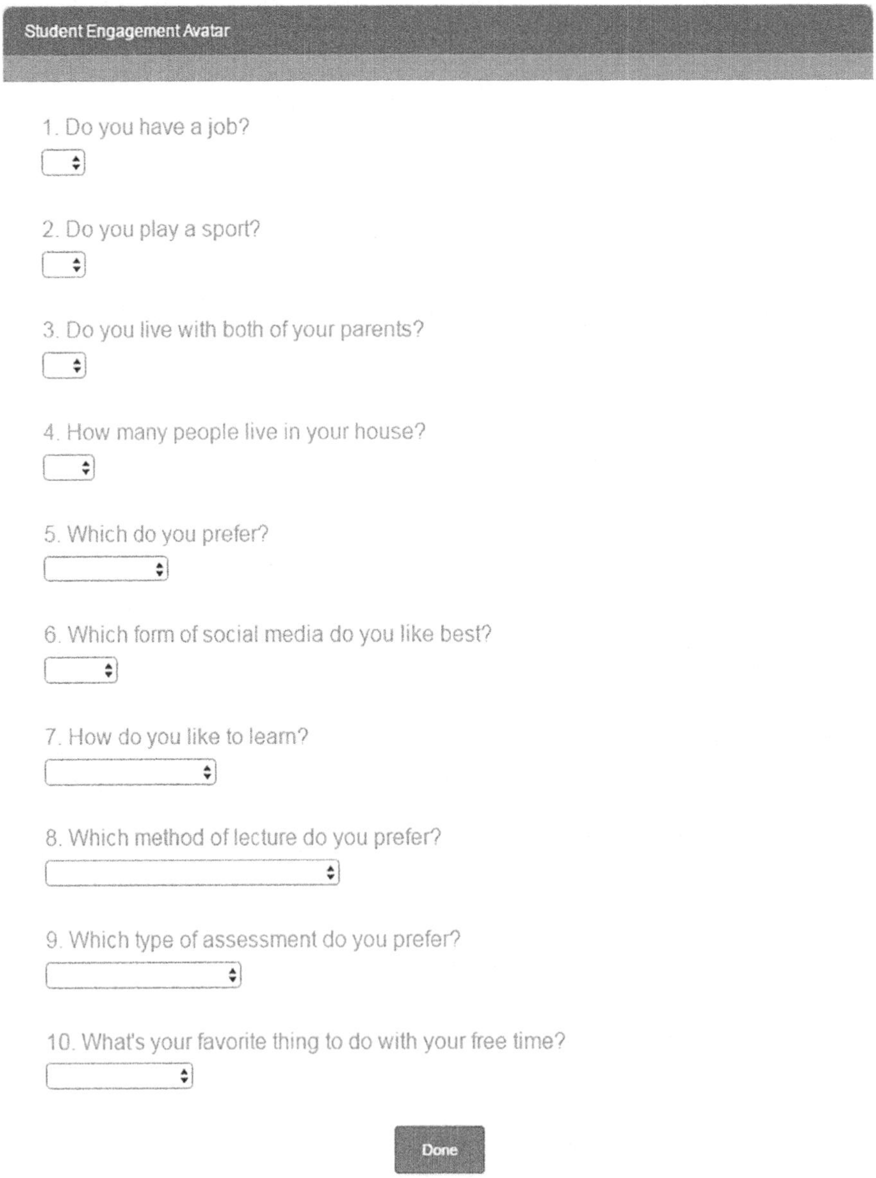
Student Engagement Avatar

1. Do you have a job?

2. Do you play a sport?

3. Do you live with both of your parents?

4. How many people live in your house?

5. Which do you prefer?

6. Which form of social media do you like best?

7. How do you like to learn?

8. Which method of lecture do you prefer?

9. Which type of assessment do you prefer?

10. What's your favorite thing to do with your free time?

Done

Image 8.1

SurveyMonkey is perfect for collecting data to create an avatar because students can answer anonymously. I've found this leads to great honesty and increased participation. SurveyMonkey then presents results in an attractive and informative fashion with bar graphs and percentages. The most popular answers to my survey become the building blocks of my student avatar. Once students submit, you'll have vital information on each learner. You can then draw on it when you personalize instruction. Perhaps a youngster loves lectures—you respond by providing this student with a podcast link. This student then joyfully listens to an expert regale her about the lesson topic. Such a learning vehicle would leave a different student cold, but not this youngster. She's in the zone. That's engagement.

You can learn even more about the power of student avatars in the *Hack Learning* podcast Episode 39 (use the QR code in Image 8.2 to get there).

Image 8.2

WHAT YOU CAN DO TOMORROW

- **Introduce the concept of an avatar.** Explain what is meant by this term. You may wish to show the trailer from the movie *Avatar* and discuss why it was titled this way.

- **Create a SurveyMonkey survey.** Ask learners basic questions that will help you build the student avatar.

- **Review the results.** Display them on your Smart Board, blog, or social channel, and talk about responses to each question. Kids find this fascinating, because ultimately it's about them.

- **Create a student response Google Form**. Provide a link to the SurveyMonkey results. Ask them to compare themselves to the emerging avatar.

- **Challenge students to bring the avatar to life.** Students could write a biography of the avatar, draw a picture of the avatar, create a Facebook page or Twitter account for the avatar.

- **Challenge the avatar**. Being like the avatar is not necessarily desirable. Prompt students to take issue with the avatar. Challenge them to list ways that being like the avatar is undesirable. Challenge them to find examples of when people challenged avatars and all of society benefitted.

- **Apply the concept outside of class**. Students could research examples of avatars in various professions, cultures, or time periods. Perhaps, students could create their own surveys and create their own avatars.

Knowing your student avatar will facilitate learner engagement. Have a blast finding your student avatar by following the directives in this hack.

HACK 9

BUILD A CLASSROOM IDENTITY AND NURTURE BELONGING

THE PROBLEM: STUDENTS DON'T HAVE ALLEGIANCE TO YOUR CLASS

I TEACH A DUAL enrollment history class. Dual enrollment is a college course taught to high schoolers. A local college or university designates high school instructors who have master's degrees in a specific subject to teach such courses. I have an MA in history, so Columbus State empowered me to teach their World Civilization class. It's been a great opportunity for our students and a lot of fun to teach. My class, however, seemed in limbo. We were still physically at Big Walnut High School, but it was a college course. So, what were we? We decided we were both...and neither. Consequently, we decided to create a unique identity.

THE HACK: CREATE A CLASSROOM IDENTITY

It's wonderful to have a sense of belonging. When you ask students about their group allegiances, they'll typically say things like:

- I'm a follower of a certain religion.

- I'm a member of my family.

- I'm an American.

- I'm an Ohioan.

- I'm a member of a political party.

41

- I'm a Cleveland Cavs fan.

- I'm a member of the softball team.

- I'm a certain gender.

- I'm a fan of a certain type of music.

- I have a certain sexual identity.

- I'm a fan of the television show *Parks and Rec*.

- I'm a member of Generation Z.

Wouldn't it be cool if students also proclaimed, "I'm a proud member of Mr. Sturtevant's class"?

You may wonder, *Why is identifying with certain groups important?* But consider this: If you identify with the television show *Parks and Rec*, when you select an episode on *Netflix*, you're automatically engaged. So it follows that if students identify with Mr. Sturtevant's class, when they enter my classroom each day, they will automatically feel a certain level of engagement.

When it came to dual enrollment World Civ, we needed a name. Big Walnut University captured the nature of our class, which is part high school and part college. It also has a nice ring to it. We amplified this newfound identity by creating a class logo to go with the name.

Image 9.1

In the middle of our class seal is the Wheel of Ashoka. Ashoka was the great Indian king who converted to Buddhism, an important topic in the course. Finally, we created class T-shirts, crewneck sweatshirts, and hoodies. All were proudly emblazoned with the Big Walnut University seal. It was like being in a fraternity or sorority without the humiliating initiation. And boy, did it draw attention and interest. My enrollment increased.

To find out more about class identity, I contacted Dr. Todd Finley of East Carolina University, who has thoroughly researched engagement. He virtually stopped by the *Hacking Engagement* podcast last summer to talk about class identity. The QR code in Image 9.2 will escort you to that broadcast.

Image 9.2

WHAT YOU CAN DO TOMORROW

- **Challenge students to come up with a unique name for your course.** Have students submit names and then the class can elect the winner.

- **Challenge students to come up with a unique logo design for your course.** Have students submit designs and then the class can elect the winner.

- **Consider ways to use a class name and logo design.** Create a letterhead or posters. Develop an online presence such as a Facebook page or Twitter account. Challenge students to create an advertising campaign.

- **Investigate the potential of creating class shirts.** My students absolutely loved this.

Challenge your students to create a class name and a class design. Vigorously promote this identity and bond students to your class. Sure, your colleagues will envy you, but that will ultimately be a good thing too, as they'll want to brand their own classes and soon engagement will soar across your building.

HACK 10

SHOW THEM WHAT'S POSSIBLE

THE PROBLEM: STUDENTS OFTEN SUFFER FROM A LACK OF VISION AND A LACK OF CONFIDENCE

I KEPT LOOKING OUT our school's huge windows on my first day of third grade. It was a beautiful late summer day. Our little elementary was surrounded by ancient hardwood maples whose leaves were pretty darned green. Just a week prior, I had been enjoying summer shirtless and barefoot. I felt sad to let summer go.

My teacher called a few students up to her desk to hand in paperwork. She told the rest of us to look through the textbooks stacked under our desks. I thought, *Wow, it has really begun.* Reluctantly, I opened my math book. I glanced through the first few chapters and it looked familiar, but then I flipped to the last chapter and was shocked. I remember thinking, *How in the world can I ever do these problems? These look like equations you'd see on a mad scientist's chalkboard in a scary movie. By the end of the year, will I really be able to do these problems?* They seemed impossible, but for the first time that day, the potential of third grade engaged me.

I want to give the young me a lot of credit because nine months later when May rolled around, we were breezing through the chapter with all those beautiful equations. I'm not impressed with my ability to master the skill; I'm impressed because I vividly remember thinking, *Wow, I never thought I'd be able to do these problems, and they're easy.*

THE HACK: SHOW STUDENTS WHAT THEY'LL BE ABLE TO DO IN THE FUTURE

In my World Civ class, students crafted Buddhist mandalas. We built these mandalas in a systematic way. In the beginning, students had zero confidence they could create a cool-looking mandala. To calm their anxiety, I displayed student examples from the previous semester. Students looked shocked because they knew many of the artists responsible for the mandalas. I typically hear, "I can't believe Maria did that," or, "Jason can't draw. Did he really do that?" This simple demonstration of others' work instills confidence.

Showing kids what's possible is a great way to instill confidence and wonder.

Invariably, one week after my demo, students present their mandalas and I hear, "I can't draw. I'm amazed I was able to do this."

When it came to math, the third-grade me needed inspiration and confidence. Your students probably need them as well. The inspiration could be like the sense of wonder I felt when I looked at advanced equations in my text, or it could be the infusion of confidence my students feel when I display student mandala examples. Regardless, inspiration of what's possible and encouragement engages, empowers, and motivates students.

WHAT YOU CAN DO TOMORROW

- **Take the unit you're studying and create an example that demonstrates what's possible.** Examples of former students' work serve this purpose well. Or, you could preview what's coming by displaying examples in the form of images, an interview in a language that students can't yet read or speak, a brief science experiment, poetry, music, artwork, or equations. Pretend you're reassuring the third-grade Jim Sturtevant on the first day of school: "You can do this. You're going to be amazed at how easy it will be."

- **Show your class an example of the concept you'll teach manifested in the adult world.** It could be a significant invention, a work of art, a corporate merger, a book jacket, an international treaty, a beautiful structure, or a Supreme Court decision.

- **Reveal the next step.** Once you've shown students what's possible, take it a step further. It could be a preview of the next unit, the next class, or perhaps a description of a career that uses the skill they'll master.

Students often need inspiration. Showing kids what's possible is a great way to instill confidence and wonder.

HACK 11

UPGRADE STUDENT GRADE CONTRACTS

THE PROBLEM: THE OLD STUDENT CONTRACT MODEL IS ANTIQUATED

I WAS A MASSIVE slacker in high school. Here were my motivations:

- School is for playing football and running track.

- School is a place to hang out with friends.

- School is where I can meet cute girls.

This was the era of direct instruction. I just wasn't engaged. I didn't feel like I had any say in my learning journey. So I focused on more interesting things that I could influence. For some odd reason, my high school academic experience came back to me while chatting with Tammy Hall, the Director of Secondary Operations at the Delaware Area Career Center in Central Ohio. At DACC, students are totally in charge of planning, implementing, evaluating, and adjusting their learning processes. I was particularly impressed with Tammy's description of personal learning plans:

> We have the advantage in vocational training of teaching learners already connected to their passions, so we can demand student ownership. Students set goals based on a six-level career matrix. They select their certification objective and then work toward that goal with our encouragement and support.

I would have had far more success in such a learning environment. My conversation with Tammy reminded me of the old concept of the grade contract. That idea has been around for as long as overhead projectors. You meet with kids, encourage them to create some appropriate academic goals, you put it in writing, and the kids sign it. It's time, however, for an upgrade with a healthy dose of technology mixed with contemporary youth inclinations.

THE HACK: UPGRADE THE GRADE CONTRACT

If you've ever studied constitutional law, you know how stupefying it is to read a contract. And yet, we often subject students to boring, unattractive grade contracts. There's nothing wrong with the intent, or the potential motivational impact, but let's strive to present such proposals in a more engaging way.

For your next class project, direct learners to create their own grade contracts on Google Forms. Mandate students to include five elements:

- A link to the rubric with an acknowledgment of understanding. Kids can copy the link from Google Classroom and paste it onto their Google Forms.

- A question that prompts students to submit their names.

- A question that prompts students to submit their grade objectives.

- A question that prompts students to submit what they consider their primary obstacles to success.

- A selfie.

Challenge students to customize their Google Form/Contract. They can change colors and adjust the layout. Suddenly, their grade contract looks a lot more like a social media page. Adding a selfie really personalizes and motivates. Putting your name on something is one thing, but attaching a selfie equates with ownership. Be prepared for images of girls doing their best duck faces and dudes flexing as if they're auditioning for *American Gladiators*.

Once they've completed the form, direct learners to share it with you for your approval. Once submitted, it's the equivalent of signing a contract.

On the due date, teachers and students can determine if the completed project jibed with the rubric and the learner's stated goals. Brainstorm with kids ways to improve their projects and then encourage them to resubmit for a higher grade.

WHAT YOU CAN DO TOMORROW

- **Display an old-school grade contract.** Ask students if they've ever used such a document.

- **Provide a rubric link.** Teachers who use Google Classroom can simply post it. If not, merely upload the rubric into your Google Drive and produce the URL link.

- **Instruct students to create their contracts.** Students create their own customized contracts and send them to the teacher for approval.

- **Direct students to send the form**. Have kids fill out their contracts and send them to themselves and you.

- **Celebrate the best in show**. Review the forms and choose five outstanding selfies and five superior customized forms. Display these to the class and have them choose the best.

Grade contracts are a valuable engagement and accountability tool. Let's make them even cooler.

HACK 12

GET TO KNOW STUDENTS THROUGH REVERSE ENGINEERING

THE PROBLEM: IT'S NOT EASY TO GET TO KNOW STUDENTS

TEACHERS ARE OFTEN lectured, "Get to know your students." That's not easy to do. A lot of kids can be pretty closed down. And, if you try to get to know them before they're ready, it can be counterproductive.

Bonding with students is fundamental to the learning process. John Hattie, in his landmark book *Visible Learning*, created a list of 138 influences on student learning. He placed student-teacher relationships in eleventh place, far ahead of many things one might think are more important.

If you've been tasked to bond with students, and you're a bit stumped on how to do it, help is on the way. Reverse engineer the problem. Instead of stalking your students and coming on too strong, entice them to come to you. In order to coax students out of their shells, or melt arctic exteriors, or win over the disruptive, teachers need to become:

- Approachable
- Intriguing
- Familiar
- Safe
- Non-threatening

THE HACK: ENGAGE STUDENTS BY BECOMING MORE APPROACHABLE

A great way to achieve approachability is to tell stories about yourself. That's right, teachers may have to come out of their shells too. Strive to become a fascinating adult who kids find compelling. Bring students into your world. Not literally—you certainly don't need to invite them to your house for dinner—but allow them to live vicariously through some of your interesting experiences. You'll be amazed at the power of this simple tactic. Allow students to get to know you. Isn't that the way you've forged other relationships?

Approachable teachers engage students and forge relationships.

Recount one of these tomorrow:

- A movie review

- Your after school routine

- A restaurant review

- A particularly challenging workout

- Your new home construction project

- A pet story

- A child story

- Details about a hobby

- The miserable performance of a favorite sports team

Image 12.1

Don't be shy. Making yourself more approachable can jump-start student engagement. To learn more about reverse engineering bonding with students, listen to the episode of the *Hacking Engagement* podcast (Image 12.1 will take you there).

WHAT YOU CAN DO TOMORROW

- **Select an experience.** This could be something simple like stopping at your favorite drive through for coffee or your wake-up routine.

- **List attributes.** Create bullet points listing why this experience was impactful. What does it say about you and your daily existence?

- **Practice a two-minute monologue about an interesting experience.** This should be something short and simple, but of a personal nature so students can learn more about you.

- **Deliver the monologue before the lesson.** This little presentation should be about one to two minutes long. Pay close attention to student reaction to your story. Record your observations. It will help you refine your future shares.

- **Prompt students.** Ask kids if they've had a similar experience. Maybe your brief share will open a door to a relationship.

Approachable teachers engage students and forge relationships. A great way to become more approachable is for teachers to tell some stories about themselves.

HACK 13

BE OBSERVANT AND FIND
THE ELUSIVE SPARK

THE PROBLEM: TEACHERS DON'T KNOW THEIR STUDENTS

TEACHERS OFTEN GET swept up in student achievement. That's totally understandable. It's one of our primary jobs. But teachers also have an obligation to foster student passion. When students pursue their passion, their spark–they're engaged. That spark is hidden in some students. Others don't even realize they have one. You can help.

THE HACK: SEARCH FOR THE SPARK IN EACH STUDENT

Become an undercover investigator. Begin your investigation early in the semester. Assign various types of hands-on activities that free you to cruise around and ask all sorts of questions, some pertaining to the activity, some geared to learning about student interests, and others focused on getting to know kids better:

- How do you like this activity?

- What's your favorite class?

- Who's your favorite teacher?

- What would you rather be doing?

- What do you like to do on the weekend?

- What's the first thing you do when you get home from school?

- What do you do well?

- How would you improve this assignment?

- How could we expand this assignment?

In addition to asking questions:

- Keenly observe them working

- Listen to what they say to one another

- Assess their products

Once you discover the spark, it'll shape how you motivate and interact with students.

As soon as you see or sense that little spark, try to confirm it: "You seem to enjoy watching YouTube. For our next unit, would you like to create a documentary about the Arab/Israeli conflict and then post it online?" It will be evident immediately if you have struck gold. If not, keep searching for the spark. The potential payoffs are huge. Through observation and friendly interrogation, you can find student sparks. Kids are intensely engaged when they pursue their passions.

WHAT YOU CAN DO TOMORROW

- **Create an activity that provides many options for expressing understanding.** Allow students to choose their method for expression. This will be an excellent first step in finding the spark.

- **Promote an example.** Tell a story of a past student who thrived once he or she started chasing a passion. Do this frequently.

- **Become a private investigator.** The subtle nature of your investigation is important in finding the spark. Students don't like being involuntary lab rats. Just observe and question in a friendly, casual way.

Once you discover the spark, it'll shape how you motivate and interact with students. Finding a student's spark and then exploiting that spark is a key to engagement. Teachers can find this spark through observation and interaction.

HASH OUT A HASHTAG

THE PROBLEM: STUDENTS RARELY THINK ABOUT YOUR CLASS OUTSIDE OF SCHOOL

Picture this, one of your students is at home watching TV. Like most multitasking teens, he is scrolling through his phone while watching. Because he follows you on Twitter, your recent post pops up on his feed.

 Sturtevantclass @sturtevantclass Apr 15
#heywc1...How about a slice of Buddha Bread with vegan butter? Can't wait 2 c what u make this weekend!

Image 14.1

He reads your tweet and laughs to himself, *Mr. Sturtevant is always putting bizarre things on our class hashtag* (see an example in Image 14.1). He likes your post, retweets it, and then remembers, *Oh yeah, I'm supposed to create a conscious eating Buddhist meal for our next blog prompt.* After reading your lighthearted electronic reminder, he waltzes into the kitchen and starts bouncing menu ideas off his mom. Mom shoots him a puzzled look, then asks him why, all of a sudden, he's interested in food prep. Instead of answering, he hands her his phone, which is displaying your class hashtag feed. She smiles as she scrolls through the tweets. She pauses on a post and then clicks on the embedded link for the Buddhist meal assignment. She reads the prompt and says, "I can see why you enjoy this class." After mother and son agree to a meal plan, your student replies to your tweet. He includes the hashtag #heywh1, so his friends will see it on the hashtag feed.

An engaging presence on Twitter can inspire kids to think, plan, and wonder about your class during their daily twenty-three-hour hiatus. It can expose your amazing classroom to grateful parents. It's time to morph your classroom into an online presence.

THE HACK: CREATE A TWITTER HASHTAG FOR YOUR CLASS

Please, if you haven't already, create a Twitter account for your class. Make it simple, but recognizable, like mine: @sturtevantclass. Think of a hashtag as an attention-grabber. Post general classroom announcements on the account feed, but if students are to reply, vote, or participate in a poll, include an attention-grabbing hashtag.

My hashtag is #heywc1. The class is World Civilization 1 and I want their attention, so I included the word "hey." Search Twitter to make sure your tag is original. If it's not, start from scratch. Here were options I considered for World Civilization 1:

- #sturtwc1
- #thesturtfeed
- #Yowc1
- #Wuzupwc1
- #attentionwc1

I like #heywc1 best. I include it on any tweet that encourages a response.

In *Hacking Engagement* podcast Episode 11 (Image 14.2), I share a story remarkably similar to my creation in this hack, including an interview with a student and a parent about the engaging nature of the activity.

Image 14.2

WHAT YOU CAN DO TOMORROW

- **Create a class Twitter account.** This will keep your professional life and private life separate, which is always smart.

- **Create a unique hashtag for your class.** Create a tag that's relatively short, but it must be unique.

- **Promote the hashtag to your students.** In the beginning you'll have to lead them. Display the hashtag on the Smart Board and encourage kids to respond. After some days of successful participation, you can foster curiosity with an offhanded comment, "Check for an interesting class hashtag prompt."

- **Share the hashtag with parents and administrators.** Most teachers have some sort of online classroom. Broadcast the hashtag to parents. Encourage them to follow you and tweet to your hashtag. Email your principal and guilt her into responding to the hashtag prompt.

- **Invite class alumni to join your hashtag.** Sturtevant veterans add to the virtual conversation immensely.

A hashtag is a fantastic way to engage kids when they're not sitting in your classroom. It also creates a unique channel that brings parents and other stakeholders inside your world.

BRING IN AN ARTIFACT FOR SHOW-AND-TELL

THE PROBLEM: STUDENTS NEED HELP ENGAGING AUDIENCES

My FIRST DAY of kindergarten was terrifying. I had to leave my home, my mom, my toys, my dog, my yard, and hang out in a chaotic room with a strange adult—my teacher. What unnerved me most were my peers. They looked huge. Would they pick on me? Could I make friends? Many of them seemed to be adjusting just fine to the new surroundings. Why was I so anxious? It was a rough few days.

Fortunately, three days into my public school experience, something magical happened. My anxiety waned and in the process, I learned valuable lessons about being an engaging educator. You heard me right. I learned to engage students as a five-year-old.

On that transformational Friday, our class had its inaugural show-and-tell session. A few of my classmates were assigned the task of bringing an artifact from home. That fateful morning, they attempted to describe their prized possession and then explain why they had brought it to share. With the exception of a pair of natural-born politicians with great stage presence, the presenters were darned nervous. I felt for each as they stammered their monologues while staring down at their feet, which were alternately sharing the burden of holding up body weight.

While their stage fright inspired empathy, what engaged me were their stories. I'll never forget this big, quiet kid. He scared me to death, but there he was, holding up a photo, mumbling about his pet cat. He certainly didn't strike me as a cat person. He seemed more the German shepherd type. An extroverted male classmate brought in his stuffed animal. *Really.* He didn't seem like the kind of kid who needed a teddy bear.

Later that day at recess, I now had the familiarity, the courage, and the curiosity to engage some of my comrades. I did just that. They were now approachable. My entire disposition toward the kindergarten enterprise improved.

THE HACK: SHOW A PERSONAL ARTIFACT AND TELL THE CLASS ABOUT IT

Bring an artifact to class, describe it, pass it around, demonstrate it, and tell kids how you got it and why it's important to you.

I love to work out, but often my muscles get tight and sore. Not long ago, I brought in a dense foam roller like the ones you see at a physical therapist's office. I demonstrated my technique for loosening my quad muscles. I lay face down with the roller under one thigh. I then moved my body back and forth as I grimaced. There's a fine line between pain and pleasure.

Students got a kick out of this bizarre demonstration. A few brave students volunteered to try my roller. This artifact inspired a wonderfully engaging experience for my students. Students entering my class later in the day asked, "Can we see your foam roller?" A student's parent who saw me in town the next day approached me to say, "You really interested my daughter with your foam roller. Where'd you get it?"

A demonstration of some simple, yet meaningful artifact from home could lead to significant engagement.

WHAT YOU CAN DO TOMORROW

- **Search your home for an interesting artifact that you could bring to class.** This artifact should inspire a brief story.

- **Describe the artifact.** Explain how you came to possess it and why it's important to you. Pay close attention to student reaction to your share. Record your observations. It will help you refine your future shares.

- **Pass it around, or let a kid try it.** Kids love to watch their classmates look ridiculous.

- **Invite students to bring in something.** Who says high school kids are too old for show-and-tell?

Bringing in an item for show-and-tell helps students get to know you. Believe it or not, kids are intrigued by their teachers, especially what they do when on shore leave.

BREAK THE ICE ICE BABY

THE PROBLEM: YOUR STUDENTS ARE CLIQUEY

THIS HAS PROBABLY happened to you at numerous PD sessions or conferences. The presenter announces that it is time to do an icebreaker. You hear a collective sigh from your comrades. Nonetheless, you comply. With slumped shoulders, you shuffle on command to a side of the room. The remainder of the participants accompany you. Together, you wait for a prompt that constitutes an assault on your dignity. Sound familiar? However much we dread these moments, the odd thing about icebreakers is that they work. You've probably bonded with strangers over your mutual disdain of icebreakers.

Icebreakers can be a valuable activity to foster class culture. A key to student engagement is for kids to feel comfortable and secure in your room, and participating in an icebreaker will speed up that process. If teachers don't use icebreakers, they're missing a golden opportunity to help kids bond. Sometimes we take it for granted that students know one another, and don't realize that this is untrue until much later in the year. Sure, when you announce an icebreaker, students will grumble a bit, but inject some humor into the situation. Enlighten kids about the activity's potential: "Who knows guys? You may just find Ms. Right in this activity. That person who sits right beside you may unveil some detail about herself that makes her irresistible." Try icebreakers to foster relationships, which will enhance the entire atmosphere of your class. Your students could become like a family. In such a positive classroom culture, engagement will flourish.

THE HACK: MAKE A LIVING MOVIE MARQUEE

Icebreakers are perfect at the beginning of each semester, before you embark on a new unit, to randomly group kids, or to create a new seating chart. This icebreaker will get kids talking and afford them the opportunity to learn fascinating things about their peers.

The *Living Movie Marquee* is easy, fun, and effective. Ask students to write down their all-time favorite movie. Have them look up the year it debuted and find some background information. They can create a virtual marquee on their devices, or go old school with paper. Encourage them to decorate their marquee with significant images, slogans, and phrases connected with the film.

> **Those improved relationships will leverage future engagement.**

Once they have their movies and the year they came out, have students drag their marquees, be they paper or virtual, into the hallway. Challenge them to form one line. All the way to the left will be the oldest movie. To the right will be the newest. Watch in delight as the students display their movie marquees to one another while arranging themselves. There will be lots of laughter and conversation. If there's a tie because movies were released the same year, you can have kids stand in a bunch, or arrange themselves alphabetically by movie title or last names.

Once they have themselves arranged, tell students they will take turns presenting their films to each other: "When it is your turn to present, step forward, turn, and face your peers; hold up the marquee; announce your favorite movie; describe any drawings or decorations on the marquee; and most importantly, explain why you love this show." There will be laughter, nods, and surprised expressions—no one knew the captain of the football team loves *Mean Girls*. Now that you have your oldest-to-newest line, it's easy to create groups in a random fashion. These groups will talk about their favorite movies all the way back to their brand new seats.

WHAT YOU CAN DO TOMORROW

- **Introduce your own marquee.** Make your own marquee the night before. Describe your marquee and why you love your favorite

> movie. Students will learn about you in the process.
>
> - **Challenge students to make their marquees.** Ten minutes is plenty of time for their creation. Once students have finished their marquees, lead them into the hall to present them to each other.
>
> - **Create a new seating chart.** Usher students back into the room to sit in their new seats with their new friends.
>
> - **Conduct a Google search.** Look for other interesting icebreakers that you can incorporate into your repertoire.

Icebreakers work. They're a blast. They foster relationships. Those improved relationships will leverage future engagement.

COLLABORATE GLOBALLY WITH VOXER

THE PROBLEM: DISENGAGED TEACHERS CAN'T ENGAGE STUDENTS

ENGAGED TEACHERS ARE engaging. This may seem self-evident, but engagement is not always easy to maintain. I've been in this gig for over thirty years: Not all of those years felt like a walk in the park. There were times I wasn't engaged either by the job or by my comrades. Fortunately, those low points were brief. You've probably been there. If you haven't, chances are you'll face some struggle with disengagement in the future. The secret to sustaining a long, fulfilling career is to keep seeking ways to keep teaching fresh, and it's awfully hard to do that in isolation.

My first book on connecting with students was published in 2014. While I'm still an obscure social studies teacher from Central Ohio, my book opened some doors, like being interviewed on podcasts. I treasure these experiences. One host transformed my professional life with a simple invitation to his Voxer group. I said, "Sure, I'd love to join." Then I went to voxer.com and learned about the voice-messaging app I had just agreed to sign up for. Using my cell phone as a walkie-talkie to communicate with a community of educators sounded neat, but I already had enough distractions in my life, and couldn't imagine using it much.

> **The walls of your school building mean nothing in this Internet age.**

But then I started voxing. The community I had joined:

- Was filled with engaging teachers who energized me

- Included hilarious people who made me laugh

- Contained ultra-supportive people

- Introduced me to the publisher of this book

- Encouraged me to create my own podcast

- Created connections that led to *Huffington Post* and *Edutopia* picking up some of my blog posts

- Taught me all kinds of ways to engage students

Voxer certainly has no monopoly on creating a forum for teachers to engage with one another, but it has served me well.

THE HACK: FIND, OR CREATE, A GROUP OF ENGAGING TEACHERS

Sign up for Voxer and search for groups you can join. Finding the right group may take time, but keep trying. Another outstanding option would be to start your own Voxer group. It's fine to invite friends to join, but your goal should be to break the bonds of geography. The walls of your school building mean nothing in this internet age. My great friend, Mark Barnes, advocates, "Teachers should use Voxer to build their tribe." I love that. My participation in Voxer has done just that, while exposing me to all kinds of opportunities to engage kids. It's been intoxicating.

WHAT YOU CAN DO TOMORROW

- **Sign up for a free Voxer account.** Voxer is certainly not the only option, but it's a good one. Like most internet tools, there's a level that's free and more features available for a price. I've been satisfied with the free level, but if you start your own group, you may wish to have more features.

- **Join a Voxer group.** Research Voxer groups and petition one for membership.

> • **Start your own Voxer group**. You could start with friends at school. Perhaps challenge them to recruit members from outside. Put out Vox prompts and group members can respond at their leisure.

Engaged teachers are engaging. Joining a group of like-minded teachers can elevate your enthusiasm, which your students will find contagious.

HACK 18

BUILD AN EXTENSIVE STUDENT SUPPORT NETWORK

THE PROBLEM: STUDENTS ARE INTIMIDATED BY ACADEMIC CHALLENGES

REMEMBER BEING CONFRONTED by an assignment that seemed impossible? Students often experience anxiety about their work. Although we all need to confront challenges to grow, facing overwhelming challenges alone can make a person feel alienated. It's counterproductive to struggle with a problem in isolation, and devastating to do so while everyone else seems fine. Students need to be assured that if they are feeling anxious, they're probably not alone.

Of course it's essential to learn how to deal with challenges—this builds resiliency and understanding. Academic vigor needs to balance against support so that students can feel the sense of accomplishment that comes with success. How about introducing simple camaraderie into your classroom?

THE HACK: ESCALATE YOUR AVAILABILITY AND
BUILD A STUDENT SUPPORT NETWORK

Michigan State researcher Kristy Cooper, in her study "Eliciting Engagement in the High School Classroom: A Mixed-Methods Examination of Teaching Practices," argues that challenging, content-focused academics can be powerfully engaging. Most kids love a challenge and thrive on a sense of accomplishment.

AP Calculus teacher Kathy Dawson certainly understands this. The students brave enough to take her class know they'll have an excellent chance of scoring a 4 or 5 on their AP test. They know that after learning from Mrs. Dawson, college math will be a breeze. There'll be times when the class seems impossible, but as long as they're willing to come in for help, Mrs. Dawson will enlighten and empower them.

> **Those improved relationships will leverage future engagement.**

Kathy Dawson elevates students by being available. Her class is populated before school, after school, at lunch, and during her conference period. Students flock to her class during their free periods because they want to understand the math. She's created a collaboration culture: "My students appreciate the invitation. They appreciate the one-on-one." If you're going to ask students to push themselves, you have to be there for them.

Obviously, you also need a work-life balance. If a student is stumped at 9:00 p.m. and you're off the educational grid enjoying your family, a powerful option is for them to turn to a peer. An even more powerful option is for them to turn to up to fourteen virtual peers simultaneously. That's the potential of a free Voxer student support group. If you have more than fifteen students, create two or three groups. When you assign something particularly challenging, create an expectation that all students will collaborate so they can ask for help from, or offer help to, peers.

Build a Kathy Dawson-like culture of collaboration in your classroom.

WHAT YOU CAN DO TOMORROW

- **Create office hours when you'll be available to help students.** You could designate your conference period, before school, after school, and even your lunch. Just make certain you can live with it. I don't have Kathy Dawson's stamina.
- **Advertise your availability.** Tell students when you're available. Encourage kids to come see you. Don't act like helping students is a burden. Be warm and welcoming.

- **Create virtual office hours.** Decide if, when, and how you'll be available when you're not at school. Consider any of the virtual tools shared in this book, as a means for communicating with students.

- **Create a peer tutoring Voxer group.** This could be comprised of up to fifteen students. It may wean them off their reliance on always coming to you for help. This could be peer tutoring at its best.

Many students find academic challenges engaging. Build a student support network to capitalize on this worthy tendency.

PRESENT FOR TEN, THEN COLLABORATE FOR TEN

THE PROBLEM: TEACHERS TALK TOO MUCH

EDUCATORS HAVE AN unquenchable thirst to explain. Like most of my colleagues, I have this urge to explain in various ways until there is no doubt in my mind that everyone understands. If students don't get it, it's my job to clarify. Unfortunately, this tendency can disengage students who got it the first time.

It's been my observation, both from the standpoint of being a student, and then working with colleagues as an adult, that teachers aren't the best at weighing the tradeoffs of their marathon explanations, presentations, and lectures. Let's be less windy. Let's become more attuned to nonverbal cues from our students. When we've lost the eyes, when their heads start to droop, when they get fidgety, when they're unresponsive to prompts, they're disengaged and we need to adjust.

Education Week contributor Peter DeWitt asks teachers four pointed questions:

1. Do you control the conversation?

2. Do students ask questions?

3. Are they allowed—even encouraged—to have conversations with one another?

4. Or do they sit as you talk?

Here are my answers:

1. *Mostly.*

2. *Yes, but I wish they'd ask more, and that more students would ask.*

3. *Some, but I don't provide enough opportunities.*

4. *Mostly.*

I have some work to do, but don't we all?

THE HACK: LOWER TEACHER VOLUME AND AMPLIFY STUDENT VOICES

This hack is comprised of two strategies to curtail teacher talk and facilitate kid talk. They can be used independently, or in concert.

The first thrust will be to limit how much you speak. You can say more with fewer words if students are engaged. Self-impose a ten-minute rule. Empower students to hold you accountable for the time limit. Say something like this: "It's 11:04. I'm going to lecture until 11:14. At that point, tell me my time is up and we will handle any questions. Then we'll do something different." You might wonder, *Why ten minutes?* Research varies on optimal presentation length. Some studies advise as little as seven minutes, while others promote up to fifteen. Ten is a nice round number and about the length of most *Ted Talks*.

The second objective is to encourage and amplify student collaboration. Keep asking yourself:

- Do I need to explain this to the entire class?

- Could students help one another explain this prompt or understand this concept?

- How can I encourage students to ask questions and express viewpoints?

Use the information that these questions generate as the basis for student interactions. Clear the middle of your class and call it "the agora." In ancient Athens, citizens met in the city square, the agora, to exchange ideas. Put five or ten minutes on the clock, and get students out of their desks and collaborating in small groups in the agora. Once the alarm sounds, have students return to their seats for debriefing. You'll interact with more engaged students who are more inclined to participate.

WHAT YOU CAN DO TOMORROW

- **Comb through your lesson.** Look over your plans to find places where you will be inclined to over-explain or talk more than you need to.

- **Decide what students can take charge of themselves.** Find some interesting topics of discussion for students to use in the agora. Look for places where students can explain ideas to one another, ask questions, and express their own viewpoints.

- **Practice the *Clear the Deck* maneuver.** Demand that students eliminate distractions. The only thing on their desks should be papers related to the class.

- **Practice the *Listen to Me with Your Face* maneuver.** Use a sweeping/gathering arm motion to command student attention. Don't start your presentation until everyone is looking at you.

- **Clear the center of the room to create the agora.** Students congregate here for collaboration. This can be done individually or in assigned small groups. Set a five- to ten-minute time limit to encourage productivity.

To engage kids, limit how much you talk. Students will fill the void with engaging collaboration.

HACK 20

RIDE THE PODCAST TIDE

THE PROBLEM: IT'S DIFFICULT TO FIND GREAT GUEST PRESENTERS

IT'S LATE MAY, and I'm looking forward to Monday. My senioritis-infected students are in for an engaging intellectual workout. Anyone who's taught eighteen-year-olds in late May probably thinks I'm crazy. And in all fairness, my seniors are developing acute cases of apathy, but I'm bringing it Monday. I have a great lesson. I'm certain I can engage them. We are studying Mesoamerica and I'm treating them to an awesome *In Our Time* BBC podcast: *The Siege of Tenochtitlan*.

You still may be skeptical. *Really? Sturtevant's students are going to enjoy a forty-minute podcast from the BBC about the fall of the Aztec capital?* The answer is *yes* and it's yes for two reasons:

- It's a gripping narrative told expertly by talented historians.
- My students will navigate fun and engaging activities that coincide with the podcast.

Anyone who has had guest presenters speak to students knows how much students get out of hearing an expert speak. It's not always easy to find someone willing or able to speak to your class about your subject matter. With the upsurge in podcasting, you can almost always find a relevant and interesting speaker online.

THE HACK: PAN FOR PODCASTING GOLD, THEN REFINE YOUR TREASURE

Please consider the pervasive nature and awesome power of the podcast. Experts from around the world are at your beck and call 24/7, and free of charge. My ninth-grade enrichment students often ask for background information for their projects. I frequently suggest NPR podcasts. I typically hear students say the next morning, "Thanks. That really helped, and it was interesting." Podcasts are mushrooming in popularity. Let's ride this tide.

Readers might wonder, *How can I find good programs?* Sign-up for iTunes and do a basic search. If your school blocks iTunes, you can easily find shows with Google. You'll soon discover that not all podcasts are worth introducing to students. I've had wonderful success with NPR programs. My forty-minute BBC podcast is much longer than I'd typically assign, but it's awesome. Many NPR shows are in the ten-minute-length range, which is great. Another powerful option is to sign up for Listenwise at listenwise.com. Listenwise is a massive sorting mechanism. If you search a topic, you'll be treated to high-quality material. If you buy a subscription, you'll gain access to outstanding lesson plans that go along with the podcasts. After you've found podcast gold, you can refine your treasure by prompting students with engaging activities.

WHAT YOU CAN DO TOMORROW

- **Give students Prime the Pump prompts.** While students listen, have them think about the content and note some thoughts so that they remember information that they can discuss or use later.

  1. Prime the Pump Prompt 1. Record something that surprised you.

  2. Prime the Pump Prompt 2. Record something new you learned.

  3. Prime the Pump Prompt 3. Record a question you desperately want answered.

- **Fill out a *Somebody wanted but so then* template.** I was interested in providing my kids with a neat tactic to organize a story or narrative. I just happened to be quite cordial with a number of English teachers, so I marched upstairs and asked them. They, rather unanimously, encouraged me to supply students with *a Somebody wanted but so then* template. I'd never heard of such a thing, so I looked it up online and found numerous options. This template is a think aloud that helps kids fill in the blanks of the story. Once they're done, the story makes sense and follows a pattern. And then, kids can go deeper!

- **Complete a character web.** While students listen, they're to complete a *Character Web* template. You can choose from a variety of templates or create your own.

- **Play Jeopardy.** While students listen, they're to create ten Jeopardy flash card questions with answers. Make five under the heading *Cool Concepts,* and five for *Name that Character.*

Podcasts are an outstanding way to deliver top-notch content. Creating engaging activities to master while students listen ensures a powerful learning experience.

EMPOWER STUDENTS TO HELP YOU UNCOVER YOUR BIASES

THE PROBLEM: TEACHERS ACCIDENTALLY ALIENATE CERTAIN STUDENTS

As a rookie teacher, I thought I had it all figured out. For some odd reason, I went out on a limb and professed a position on a controversial subject to my kids. As I bellowed my views, I was inspired by a lot of nodding. There was no doubt the majority were thoroughly on board. I could sense them thinking, *Go Mr. Sturtevant. We're with you.*

I was shocked, however, when a student confronted me after class. This young lady, while a good student, always seemed standoffish. But she was anything but aloof on this day: "Mr. Sturtevant, you should be careful about promoting your views so passionately. I don't agree with you, and I'm not alone."

While this interaction unnerved me, my ego was still invested in my position. After she left, an intense sinking feeling suddenly drained my body. It was truly an epiphany. Of course my student was right. I was erecting barriers between us. Why in the world would I alienate certain kids who may not agree with me on a certain issue?

THE HACK: CREATE A TEACHER DISPOSITION ASSESSMENT

A Teacher Disposition Assessment (TDA) measures bias. Student experts, who consume your presentations daily, generate critical information. The TDA is a set of teacher-created prompts based on potentially controversial subjects that may surface in the course content. A TDA is a fantastic exit ticket at the end of a semester, but it can be used anytime. Creating the TDA on a form creation platform like SurveyMonkey is awesome because student responses are anonymous. Plus, learners can see how their classmates responded collectively. SurveyMonkey displays results with colorful bar graphs.

Student responses provide wonderful insights.

I teach a World Civilizations class. Here's one of my TDA item prompts:

"Muslims should be restricted from entering the United States."

A. Mr. Sturtevant strongly agrees

B. Mr. Sturtevant somewhat agrees

C. Mr. Sturtevant somewhat disagrees

D. Mr. Sturtevant strongly disagrees

E. Mr. Sturtevant's opinions on this issue are unclear

It's fine to be provocative; such statements will engage your audience. Student responses provide wonderful insights. This hack could help you dramatically in the engagement department. You may be shocked by what you learn. You may have to make adjustments in your statements and actions, but that's the idea behind the TDA.

WHAT YOU CAN DO TOMORROW

- **Craft a list of "loaded" topics.** These are potential content bombshells that frequently emerge during a semester.

- **Create a Teacher Disposition Assessment (TDA).** This assessment will be comprised of controversial statements about topics in your content. Students will try to determine your disposition toward such statements.

- **Conduct a post-assessment debriefing.** You could learn much from student feedback. Share the overall responses to the TDA and ask students what it says about you and their perceptions of you.

- **Empower students to act as consultants**. After they've completed the TDA and participated in the debriefing, share an anonymous Google Form where they can give you advice and feedback. Note: you can create a Google Form like this in less than five minutes.

- **Prompt students to reflect.** Ask students to monitor their statements and actions over the next twenty-four hours. Perhaps this activity will influence their behavior as well. It could lead to some fascinating conversation the next day.

You can't engage all students if you're biased. A Teacher Disposition Assessment will help you make adjustments and bond with kids.

HACK 22

CHALLENGE STUDENTS TO SOLVE A MYSTERY

THE PROBLEM: OPINIONATED TEACHERS REPEL MANY LEARNERS

CONTENTIOUS NATIONAL AND state elections are tricky. Students want to know how their teachers vote. But one sure-fire way to alienate portions of your class is to be too blustery about your opinions. Instead, embrace elections as a fantastic opportunity to engage students. This hack will be an amazing teachable moment for students and teachers. It will also be a lot of fun.

It's okay for teachers to be a little mysterious. It's best to keep certain attributes, like having multiple spouses, or working undercover for the CIA, shrouded in mystery. It's also wise to play close to the vest in regard to religious affiliation, political party preference, and whether you inhaled in college. You don't want to be such a completely open book that a few of your students want to slam the book shut, or tear out some pages. The next time a student asks who you are voting for, view it as an awesome engagement opportunity.

THE HACK: CHALLENGE LEARNERS TO SOLVE THE TEACHER PREFERENCE MYSTERY

Here's a great way to respond to questions about voting preference: "What's your guess?" Such a prompt will probably inspire other students to jump into the conversation and generate predictions. Just be cool in the face of this onslaught. Like a pompous press secretary, don't give an inch. After they've exhausted their inquiries, pose this challenge: "I'm not going to tell you whom I'm voting for, I want you to try and figure it out. The election is a month away. Listen to everything I say, and how I say it. Search for other, more subtle clues. On election day, everyone needs to give me a prediction and an explanation for how they think I'll vote. This will be a great test for you to uncover bias. It'll also be useful for me in my quest to be fair and objective."

Solving this mystery will engage students. It will challenge kids to listen, look, and evaluate. They can then apply these investigative skills to candidates and media reports outside of the classroom. It will also help teachers in their quest to be fair, objective, and open-minded to all students regardless of their creeds. Incidentally, once the election is over and students have submitted their predictions with rationales, a teacher still doesn't have to come clean.

WHAT YOU CAN DO TOMORROW

- **Select a controversial issue.** Generally, students are very tuned into presidential elections, but they also can be passionate about gubernatorial races and controversial state issues. You could also conduct this hack in a non-election year with any controversial issue. It's essential that both you and your students care about it.

- **Plan how you can avoid giving away your position.** Think about how you've addressed controversial issues in the past. What adjustments can you make to your presentation?

- **Introduce the challenge.** It's best if a student prompts you, but it's fine for you to start the process.

- **Provide an example of bias.** Display how two news organizations with very different agendas report the same story. You could compare MSNBC and FOX. Prompt students to speculate what the different reporting says about each organization's motives.

- **Challenge students to find examples of bias.** Kids can search in the media, the statements and actions of other staff members, or the statements and actions of friends and family. Real-world applications such as this encourage engagement.

Contentious issues offer a wonderful engagement opportunity. Challenge students to solve the teacher preference mystery.

BECOME A GRAND INQUISITOR

THE PROBLEM: TEACHER QUESTIONS ARE OFTEN ARBITRARY AND INEFFECTIVE

OVER THE PAST thirty years, Penny Sturtevant has been a science teacher, a guidance counselor, an assistant principal, and a principal. Next year, she'll work at the district level. Oh…she's also my wife. Penny has observed her share of lessons. When I asked how to engage with students, she responded immediately with, "*Questions.*" Quite simply, Penny believes that questioning students is an essential art that can be mastered with practice.

Asking engaging, creative questions, at key junctures in a lesson, is transformational. Such questions act as formative assessments, but more importantly, open doors to deeper understanding. Thought-provoking questions elevate kids on Bloom's Taxonomy Pyramid.

I've observed teachers ask a good question, but then not allow the kid the time to formulate a response. I've watched other instructors ask a question, and then nervously answer it themselves without giving the student a chance. You have to be patient and let the answer evolve. Sometimes teachers ask questions that demand a regurgitation of trivial facts. These questions have no depth; they're boring to listen to and answer, which leads to student disengagement. Obviously, there are times when you have to ask such questions. There are times when facts, data, or yes or no answers are required, but they certainly shouldn't dominate. Questions have more potential than just rote responses. Don't poison the well with too many drab prompts!

Even though most teachers would agree that the quality of questions integrated into a classroom has a direct impact on the quality of the education that students receive, poor questioning is still a common feature of many practices.

THE HACK: IMPLEMENT EXCELLENT QUESTIONING

Asking great questions is part of the equation. It's also essential to ask them strategically. Penny believes asking dynamic questions can be compared to an art form. Let's say tomorrow your students are working in small groups. Formulate questions this evening in preparation. Use Bloom's Taxonomy Pyramid as your question creation template and aspire to climb to the apex. Here are a few sample questions you can use:

Penny elaborates on the power of questions on the Hacking Engagement Podcast, accessible with your QR reader via Image 23.1.

Analyze: "How can you demonstrate the difference between a plant and animal cell?"

Evaluate: "Which is better, reading an eBook, or a physical book? How could you convince others of your choice?"

Create: "You're required to teach a peer about the Han Dynasty. What could you produce to enlighten your classmates?"

Also, stock your quiver with questions that can help kids hit the target if they get stymied:

- Are there any advantages to eBooks?

- Why is the Han Dynasty so significant?

- How are plant and animal cells the same?

Great questions will help determine if kids are on point. Not only should teachers create these questions, but they should also decide when they are going to ask them and how they'll behave when students respond.

WHAT YOU CAN DO TOMORROW

- **Evaluate your essential questions.** Each lesson should be driven by a few essential questions. Evaluate these questions, or if necessary, take a step back and determine what they are.

- **Create a handful of follow-ups.** Each essential question should inspire more questions. Create and list those. This will be your arsenal, your script. Follow-up questions can deepen learning.

- **Review your seating chart.** Certain students love when you ask them a question and will freely elaborate. Other students fall more into the wallflower category. The goal is to draw out all types, inspire all students to express their thinking. You could even highlight your seating chart. Being aware of student expression inclinations will help you to ask questions strategically. You'll know where to look, stand, move to, and avoid. If there's strong discussion momentum, prompt a wallflower. If the discussion needs an infusion of energy, ask an extrovert. Ensure that everyone participates.

- **Decide where and how you'll unleash questions in tomorrow's lesson.** Remember, questioning is an art form. Plan what you'll ask, how you'll ask, and when you'll ask. You'll still have wonderful questions that emerge organically. In fact the better you get at asking awesome questions, magically, more and more questions will materialize.

- **Encourage students to formulate questions.** Q & A should never be a one-way street.

Essential questions are merely a starting point. Engage learners by going deeper with irresistible questions asked in a strategic manner.

HACK 24

DARE KIDS TO WRITE ON A VIRTUAL BULLETIN BOARD

THE PROBLEM: YOU NEED A NEW, FUN, AND VISUALLY APPEALING WAY FOR STUDENTS TO EXPRESS THEMSELVES

I HAVE TO CONFESS, I do try to up my game for evaluations. Be honest—don't you? I recently tried something for an evaluation. My lesson was the Israeli-Palestinian conflict, which I was teaching to ninth graders. The class was equally divided, with each half assigned to promote either the Palestinian or Israeli perspective. At a strategic juncture in the lesson, students were to express justifications as to why their adopted group should occupy and govern the disputed terrain. I wanted this phase to be ultra engaging, so I was hoping to explore new avenues for student expression.

When I prompted the group of colleagues I connect with on Voxer for ideas about a more interesting way for students to express themselves, they responded big time. Their best suggestion was to encourage kids to post on a virtual bulletin board.

THE HACK: STUDENTS EXPRESS THEMSELVES ON A VIRTUAL BULLETIN BOARD

This hack is simple and straightforward but also powerful. Think of a lesson that calls for student expression. Create some prompts that will elicit a response. Then teach students to use a virtual bulletin board application, which allows learners to express themselves while simultaneously reading posts from classmates.

Two fantastic web applications that you can use to build bulletin boards are Padlet and TodaysMeet. Whichever one you choose to use, introduce students to the conventions of the app and give them guidelines for how and what to post. All students should be required to post. Their contributions can be simple statements, images, or media files. Kids read or watch posts from their classmates on their Chromebooks or phones and then respond. The classroom Smart Board acts like a jumbotron. All posts appear for everyone to see and read.

When learners express themselves they're engaged

The virtual bulletin board activity was a hit during my evaluation. Engagement in our classroom blossomed as kids scrambled to hit the send button in the brief time they had to express. I sneaked a peek at my principal in the back. He was staring intently at his laptop and then up at the Smart Board, reading student submissions with a broad smile on his face. Posting on a virtual bulletin board has become a common form of student expression in my class.

WHAT YOU CAN DO TOMORROW

- **Explore TodaysMeet.** TodaysMeet is similar to Twitter in that posters are allotted 140 characters. Because they are familiar with its format, many kids are ultra comfortable with TodaysMeet.

- **Explore Padlet.** Padlet is more visually appealing and permits more expression in terms of post length and attachments. As a result, messages are a little harder to digest quickly, but the format looks cool.

- **Create a provocative prompt.** It could be something very simple like a bell ringer, or a formative assessment question. Think of a prompt that students will not be able to ignore.

- **Encourage learners to interact with one another.** When students post statements, other kids sometimes reply. When kids post questions, classmates often can't resist responding.

- **Debrief students.** Ask students what they thought about expressing in this fashion. Ask them their opinion of your prompts. Solicit their advice on how you could make the activity more engaging.

When learners express themselves they're engaged. Virtual bulletin boards give kids a chance to shout out their ideas in a really cool way.

HACK 25

LIBERATE EXCEPTIONAL STUDENTS

THE PROBLEM: ADVANCED STUDENTS OFTEN
GET BORED IN REQUIRED CLASSES

IT CAN BE humbling to teach a brilliant student. You might wonder, *Do I have anything to offer this kid?* Rest assured, you do, but it may involve unleashing them.

Anna Cryan is one of those brilliant students. She absorbs everything. She has a remarkable capacity to grasp and synthesize information. On top of that, she has the ability to abstract. She gets subtlety. Anna watched, enjoyed, and then wrote an outstanding movie review of *Dr. Strangelove* as a Cold War enrichment activity. That's hardly a movie on a typical fourteen-year-old's Netflix watch list. This is one impressive high school freshman. In her ten years of public education, Anna has sat through numerous lessons she probably could have taught more effectively than the teacher.

A kid like Anna feels most engaged when she has autonomy. Here's how she described a project she loved in sixth grade:

> We were given freedom. We weren't tied to a strict rubric so that everyone had the exact same project and the exact same thing to say. There weren't dozens of restrictions to hold students back. This project really encouraged both creativity and learning because it wasn't only a presentation, or only a creative representation. It challenged and engaged all my classmates.

If you want your high-fliers to soar, you have to stop delimiting their boundaries. Give them freedom to do work that genuinely interests them.

THE HACK: CREATE A SEPARATE SPACE FOR ENRICHMENT

You'll engage your Annas if you view every topic as a springboard. If it's quite clear from a pre-assessment that a student already gets it, go ahead and liberate her. If you use an online application like Google Classroom, use it as a virtual classroom for your high performers. Create a separate section on Google Classroom. Find or write challenging, engaging prompts for every unit and store them in the "Enrichment" section so that students who have already mastered the basics can push themselves further. Issue invite codes to students who already get what's being taught in the lesson.

Offer enrichment to everyone, not just the high fliers. I give all my students the opportunity to take part in enrichment activities. Other teachers may balk at this, which I totally understand. If kids express a willingness to try an enrichment program, I freely give them the Google Classroom invite code to unlock the enrichment prompt. I've had students that I never would have approached individually do marvelous work.

WHAT YOU CAN DO TOMORROW

- **Analyze a pre-assessment.** This tool will help you identify learners who may already know the material in the next unit.

- **Create a list of students who seem capable but bored by traditional instruction.** These students are capable of so much more than they can demonstrate if they have to work at the same pace other students do.

- **Approach learners individually.** Mention to students who scored well on the pre-assessment and to students who seem capable but disengaged that today you'll present them with an option that will excite them.

- **Create a challenging prompt for the unit you're currently studying.** You may wish to give students options in how they respond. They could write a paper, do a presentation, create an artifact or poem, produce a video or a podcast. Regardless of the form it takes, the objective will be to engage students through higher-level thinking.

Some students are disengaged because the material is not challenging, or traditional instruction leaves them cold. Liberate these students by creating a classroom within your classroom. Here, they'll have freedom to explore, learn, and express.

ENGAGE THE ENRAGED

THE PROBLEM: YOU HAVE AN OBNOXIOUS STUDENT WHOSE RADICAL VIEWS WOULD CAUSE GENGHIS KHAN TO BLUSH

TEACHING IS ODDLY like attending a family reunion on a daily basis. There are certain kids you can't wait to see every morning. Conversation with them is effortless. Your interactions are filled with smiles, nods, and laughter. But your classes aren't just comprised of your hilarious uncle or your fascinating cousin. Unfortunately, there are also ultra-annoying students who make you cringe when they amble into your room. You might think of them as your annoying extended family member whose loud rants ruin everyone's holiday.

You love almost everything about Thanksgiving. You catch up with family, eat and drink like you're attending a Greek symposium, watch some meaningless football, and enjoy not being a teacher for a day. Everything is copacetic until you're tardy to the dinner table. That's bad news. Your only option is to sit next to Uncle Archie. Uncle Archie resides in the basement and only surfaces for family events. He's a bigoted know-it-all. If he button-holes you at a gathering, you're in for a rough stretch of highway. You're now confronted with a meal filled with conspiracy theories and racist and sexist rants that belong in the deep recesses of the previous century. The holiday ambiance is destroyed.

Teachers need to engage *all* their students.

Enduring a meal with a maniac is painful, but it's just

one meal. Imagine an adolescent version of Uncle Archie striding into your class. Now, you're confronted with the daily drudgery of interacting with a very biased Archie Jr. who, just like his namesake, is quick to profess bizarre theories. Most important, the captive audience—the remainder of your students—will be subjected to these monologues too.

But your new student isn't your crazy uncle. You simply *must* engage him: That's your job. This obligation may seem distasteful, but flip your paradigm and embrace this as an amazing learning opportunity. This difficult student will be your teacher. He'll expose your biases, your triggers, and your limited perspectives. He'll engage your empathy, your objectivity, and your fair-mindedness.

THE HACK: ENGAGE YOUR MOST CHALLENGING STUDENTS

Your mantra moving forward is: *I'm going to bond with this kid.* Here are some ways you can attempt to engage a difficult student:

- Initiate casual conversation about non-controversial topics.

- Smile frequently.

- Greet the student warmly whenever possible.

- Offer compliments when the student deserves them.

- Take an interest in what the student does outside of school.

- Offer more effective and appropriate ways to express ideas.

- Keep your cool when the student spouts something disgusting.

Remember, the focus is to bond with this kid, not to pound your chest and put him in his place. The problematic student, the rest of the class, and you will all reap benefits if you can act dispassionately and manage to engage him. The student will begin to succeed academically and socially; your class will have a calmer, more congenial atmosphere for learning; you will confront your biases and become more empathetic.

If you teach for any amount of time, you'll be confronted with an opinionated or inappropriate student who knows how to push your buttons. Engage him. Who knows, you may just end up with a new young friend.

WHAT YOU CAN DO TOMORROW

- **List attitudes or dispositions you detest.** I struggle with kids who promote absurd conspiracy theories, exhibit racist or elitist attitudes, or spread malicious gossip. Whenever I have to deal with a kid who fits one of these categories, my patience gets tested. Compose your own list so you'll be prepared when you encounter a student who will exercise your stamina.

- **Pinpoint the difficult students on your roster.** You'll certainly have a couple of students who yank your chain. Commit yourself to engaging those kids. You'll serve their best interests, provide a positive atmosphere for your other students, and potentially make your job a thousand times more enjoyable.

- **Practice holding your tongue.** Tomorrow, when a student does something that tries your patience, don't react in the typical way. Mute your words and your body language. Breathe through the experience if necessary. This will help you in your relationship with this young person and can also be quite therapeutic.

- **Empathize.** When you consider a young pot-stirrer, ask yourself: *Why does she do or say such things? What's his background?* This simple empathetic moment could be a breakthrough in your ability to deal with and then eventually bond with this youngster.

Engagement is not just about getting kids to pay attention, it's also about relationships. Teachers need to engage *all* their students. Obnoxious, confrontational, or irrational students present a huge challenge in this department, but they offer tremendous opportunities for growth.

HACK 27

BUST DOWN THE WALLS OF YOUR CLASSROOM

THE PROBLEM: THE CONFINING NATURE OF YOUR CLASSROOM IS A DRAG

Getting out of your classroom for a lesson can spark student interest. Students get used to even the most engaging teacher after a while, and long for variety in their routines. As a district instructional coach, Jason Manly loves when teachers come to him with a vision of what they want to do in class and ask him, "How can I use technology to make this lesson pop?" Jason has a reputation for creativity and responsiveness. If you ask him how to expand outside your classroom walls, he's ready with a fabulous hack.

Students become engaged when a teacher stokes their curiosity, uses technology, incorporates physical movement, fuels their competitive fires, and encourages a little teamwork. That's pretty impressive for one hack.

THE HACK: CREATE A SCAVENGER HUNT USING THE ENTIRE SCHOOL BUILDING

If you've ever watched the ancient TV series *Mission Impossible* or its more recent movie franchise, you'll be totally down with this hack. Jason elaborates: "As a former Health and P.E. teacher, I like to incorporate learning activities that include movement, so I developed this challenge for a professional development session." Jason created a *Mission Impossible* themed scavenger hunt to use as an assessment review.

The activity started with a grainy video of a shadowy person giving a brief

111

explanation of the mission. Each participant or group was then given an envelope with a different prompt. After each group solved their prompt, they destroyed the message and approached the teacher with the solution. The teacher then provided a clue to locate the next prompt, which was a QR code located or posted subtly somewhere in the building. Each QR code, or stop along the scavenger hunt, contained a problem to solve.

Students collaborated, solved the problem, and then emailed the teacher their solution. Email was necessary because the students were scattered throughout the building. If their solution was correct, the instructor congratulated kids on their teamwork and provided a crucial hint as to where to find the next QR code.

The scavenger hunt contained numerous stops, but students didn't have to visit stops in the same order. The goal was to be the first group to find all the QR codes and solve all the prompts.

Image 27.1

It's one thing to read about Jason's scavenger hunt, but you'll truly be sold on the process once you try it for yourself. Why not jump right in? Aim your QR code reader on Image 27.1.

If you create a similar *Mission Impossible* scavenger hunt, student engagement will be off the hook.

WHAT YOU CAN DO TOMORROW

- **Download a QR code scanner.** There are plenty of free options. Search QR code reader or navigate to i-nigma.com. Have students download scanners if they do not already have them.

- **Create a QR code.** There are plenty of free options. Search for "QR code generator."

- **Scout your building.** Find some interesting locations for QR codes. Try to make certain your codes won't be damaged or removed. You may want to make a number and hope at least some survive the day.

- **Break a lesson into steps**. Take what you're teaching tomorrow and break it into sections. Create a problem or question related to each of the sections. These will be the stops along the scavenger hunt. The final destination should be back at your room—home base.

- **Commission student guides.** Select a cadre of students to act as scavenger hunt guides. They can aid wayward search parties. These kids should have a deep understanding of the lesson. This will be peer teaching in a very creative fashion.

Sometimes the classroom gets stale. Set up a scavenger hunt that uses the entire school building. Add energy, fun, and movement, three key ingredients of engagement to tomorrow's lesson.

HACK 28

GO AHEAD AND BE FLIPPANT

THE PROBLEM: STUDENTS ARE DISENGAGED AND DOWNRIGHT FIDGETY

I THOROUGHLY INVESTED MYSELF in my discipline of history during college. But even a history geek like me struggled during marathon lectures. And you should've seen my classmates—class often looked like a massacre. I remember thinking, *This is an awfully passive way to learn. I could read what he's saying in a book.* In the midst of those lectures I felt like a prisoner with no control. And remember, I was a guy who loved history.

This is relevant because I teach dual enrollment history to high school juniors and seniors. A few years ago, my principal asked me to teach dual enrollment, which brings college courses to the high school campus. I was initially reluctant because the sponsoring college had made clear its expectation that lecture would form a major portion of the class. I remembered my comatose classmates back in college. I didn't want to do that to my kids.

Regardless of my hesitancy, I signed on. My challenge was to make lectures engaging. I certainly wasn't going to stand in front of the class and drone on. I decided to try something new.

THE HACK: CREATE A FLIPPED PRESENTATION

I flipped my classroom by having students access lectures on video at home so that we could use class time for more active learning experiences. I record a lecture, upload it to YouTube, and then make it available to students. I use Moovly as the platform to create my flipped lectures. I then post the YouTube link on my Google Classroom page so students can access it. The benefits of this tactic are extensive. Here are some reasons flipping a lecture engages students:

Student reaction has totally sold me on the engagement potential of flipped lectures.

- They watch the video at home on their own time.

- In class the next day, they apply what they learned in an active way and the teacher is free to help if they have questions.

- They are accustomed to watching YouTube videos.

- They can stop your presentation and rewind if they missed something.

- The flipped lecture empowers students.

It's essential, however, that you work very hard to make your flipped lectures engaging. Just because it's a video doesn't mean it'll automatically interest students.

Image 28.1

Image 28.1 provides you with a link to one of my lectures if you'd like an example.

Student reaction has totally sold me on the engagement potential of flipped lectures. One student told me, "I prefer the flipped lecture because watching videos is what my generation does." The challenge for teachers then becomes making engaging flipped lectures. Please give it a try.

WHAT YOU CAN DO TOMORROW

- **Choose a presentation to flip.** Start small with a presentation that is about five minutes long.

- **Select a number of public domain images.** Images will bring your flipped presentation to life. Please respect copyright laws and use public domain images—there are plenty available. Also, don't get stuck in the box of thinking you need an exact image match to what you're studying. If you're presenting on ancient Sparta, instead of obsessing over finding images of Spartan warriors, look up images that portray dedication, intensity, or strictness.

- **Record the lecture and then upload it to YouTube.** You can screen-record a PowerPoint or a Prezi. You could create a presentation on Moovly. Regardless of how you capture your lecture, save it to a video file and then upload it to YouTube.

- **Have students apply what they've learned the next day in class.** It's smart to have students prove they watched the video. It could be as simple as showing that they took notes for a completion grade. After they've proved they watched the video, get them busy applying the content.

Watching videos is what this generation does. So when in Rome, do as the Romans do and upload your engaging flipped lecture to YouTube. This format empowers students to be self-directed.

BECOME A PROPONENT OF THE EXPONENT

THE PROBLEM: STUDENTS ARE DISENGAGED IN MATH CLASS

I HAVE TO CONFESS, when Zach Hite enthusiastically marched into my room to share a math challenge, I was ambivalent. I barely survived math. During my formative years, I was one of those students who asked the question math teachers dread most: "When are we ever going to use this stuff?"

Now that I'm an adult and a colleague to many math teachers, like Zach, I've developed great respect for what they do. Student engagement is a huge burden for math teachers. Even so, Zach surprised me with his challenge. He unveiled a cool way to engage math students. And, this hack could be used in any subject.

THE HACK: CAPTIVATE YOUR STUDENTS WITH A BACKSTORY ABOUT A COMPLICATED TOPIC

Okay, enough teasing, here's Zach's *Cubic Triples Challenge*:

Find whole number values of a, b, and c that make the following equation true:

$$a^3 + b^3 = c^3$$

For example, you might guess a = 3, b = 4 and c = 5, but those numbers don't work:

$3^3 + 4^3 = 5^3$ does not work because $3^3 + 4^3 = 91$, and $5^3 = 125$,

and 91 does not equal 125.

So, can you find other values that *do* work?

After Zach's description of the challenge, I was still just moderately engaged. It was interesting, but it didn't captivate me until he told me the story behind the equation:

> In 1637, Frenchman Pierre de Fermat made the bold claim that this problem has no solution. You could make a different guess every second for the next million years, and none of your guesses would ever work. Fermat made this claim in 1637, but he never explained *why* the problem is impossible. Giving a logical argument (proving) that the problem was impossible was a problem in itself. Countless mathematicians worked on it for hundreds of years. The first successful explanation was created by Andrew Wiles in 1994.

Zach's story got me. Now, I was curious. Now, I was engaged. Oh, by the way, Andrew Wiles proved Fermat correct. Zach's students had the same reaction when they heard the backstory. They were engaged and eagerly accepted the challenge.

Humans are wired to respond to stories. Finding an intriguing backstory about some aspect of your curriculum will excite student curiosity and make academic challenges appealing.

WHAT YOU CAN DO TOMORROW

- **Select a topic in your curriculum that's difficult for students to grasp.** Math teachers are certainly not alone in lulling their students into a stupor.

- **Research the backstory of the topic you select.** How was it formulated? When was it formulated? What conditions contributed to its formulation? What are some interesting tidbits of information?

- **Present the backstory in a compelling way.** You could tell a brief story before introducing the topic, or assume the identity of a character in the backstory and have students ask you questions.

- **Challenge students to find backstories.** Perhaps the kids can find interesting stories for you. Give them a topic and tell them to dig in.

- **Direct students to dramatize a backstory**. After they uncover fascinating narratives pertaining to your lesson, challenge students to act out skits to engage and inform their classmates.

Teachers can generate engagement by using narratives related to complex topics. Such stories are wonderful ways to introduce topics and can lead to outstanding forms of student expression.

AVOID THE GREAT WAR ON YOGA PANTS

THE PROBLEM: YOU'RE ALIENATING STUDENTS BY BATTLING POWERFUL SOCIAL TRENDS

IN 1969 MY sister was a junior in high school. I was proud of my older sibling when she participated in a student protest. No, it wasn't about the Vietnam War. No, it wasn't about civil rights. It was about pants. You see, at our very typical public high school the dress code required girls to wear longish skirts or dresses. Wearing slacks, not jeans mind you, but dress slacks, was considered too "masculine." From the vantage point of the twenty-first century, such a policy seems ridiculous, but back in '69 it was serious business. I remember hearing an incensed mom say, "If we relax our rules on proper dress, girls will start dressing like prostitutes and the boys won't be able to concentrate." I asked my brother, "What's a prostitute?"

I've witnessed titanic shifts in school policies because of social trends. By the time I graduated from high school in 1979, everyone wore jeans and T-shirts to school. As a young teacher in the '80s, I was grateful when schools finally stopped expelling girls who were pregnant. I watched colleagues freak out about students listening to Walkmans in the hallways. More recently, I've witnessed teachers having conniptions over the invasive nature of the omnipresent cell phone. The truth is, social trends generally fuel terrific school policy disputes. Teachers risk appearing like out-of-touch relics to their students if they swim strenuously against the strong tides of culture. One example of this phenomenon is the recent brouhaha over girls wearing yoga pants.

A few years ago our administration got exercised over the yoga pants epidemic. Perhaps because I'm a dude and I don't care much about dress code, it was tough for me to get excited about the banning yoga pants crusade. I watched the battle unfold instead of participating in the combat. It was fascinating. The conservative forces of the status quo lost big-time. They got buried under an avalanche of spandex. I knew the war was lost when I went to a basketball game and saw bleachers full of thirty- and forty-something moms sporting yoga pants. I recently commented to my students, "Girls, when it came to yoga pants, you just wore everyone down." A proud young female nodded and said, "We sure did."

THE HACK: EVALUATE WHETHER YOUR CLASSROOM POLICIES ARE IN NEED OF AN UPDATE

This is a simple but a profound hack. Examine each of your classroom procedures. If you haven't changed them for many years, this review is highly advisable. Ask yourself these questions:

- How does this procedure benefit students?

- Is this procedure enforceable?

- Does this procedure take into account powerful social trends?

If you have procedures inspired by another era or ones that discount powerful social trends, you're disengaging from your students.

Instead of wondering, find out what students think. I'm a huge fan of SurveyMonkey. This easy and free online tool allows kids to express themselves anonymously. My classroom policy survey was an epic conversation starter. If you want to talk engagement, give students a survey like the one in Image 30.1. It's comprised of six basic questions with a text-box for student opinions. My survey elicited numerous passionate rants.

How's our School out of Step?

1. Indicate a school rule that is out of touch with your generation.

[   ]

2. Why do you think our school has this rule?

[   ]

3. What would be a better policy?

[   ]

4. What's a rule in Mr. Sturtevant's class you'd like to see changed?

[   ]

5. Why do you think Mr. Sturtevant has this rule?

[   ]

6. What would be a better policy?

[   ]

Done

Image 30.1

WHAT YOU CAN DO TOMORROW

- **Create a survey about school and classroom policies.** You can make it short, like my six-question example. Provide a text-box for student responses. Interesting responses will stoke the conversational flames.

- **Play devil's advocate.** Make it clear you're playing this role. Indicate that you're just trying to present both sides and you may or may not agree with the position you're advocating.

- **Encourage and amplify student voices.** Challenge students to analyze policies from outside the classroom. Encourage them to express their concerns to policy-makers. They might write a column, create a cartoon, craft a petition, build a collage, or write a letter to a decision maker. They can advocate for or against changing a policy.

Teachers undermine student engagement when they cling stubbornly to out-of-date policies. Let them help you out of the abyss.

HACK 31

TRANSCEND TRANSIENCE

THE PROBLEM: KIDS MOVE IN, THEN A MONTH LATER THEY MOVE OUT

THE HEART OF John Hattie's book *Visible Learning* is a list of 138 influences on student learning. At the very bottom of this list, in 138th place, is student mobility, when students change schools frequently, often in the midst of the school year. You've probably had a child move into your class one month only to disappear by the next. This lack of continuity can be devastating to that child's intellectual development.

Unfortunately, student mobility is a reality for many kids in poor urban districts. Such schools typically suffer from poor student attendance as well. Kelly Bloomer certainly understands this. She's a high school assistant principal, but spent many years teaching in a poor district that contended with serious attendance and transience issues:

> Challenge the student to create a topic that will help the community but still be relevant to the curriculum.

The biggest obstacles to engaging our students were truancy, attendance, and transience. When we measured student performance on standardized tests, the kids that started at our school as kindergarteners and stayed with us did just fine. The students who struggled came and left, came and left, and came and left. Unfortunately, at our school, many students fell into that transient category. Poverty fuels poor attendance and transience. Child custody frequently switched, so kids would have to move.

Many families couldn't afford the rent and would have to move. Many of our kids worked so their families could survive. Academics is often not a priority in such a situation.

THE HACK: CREATE A SERVICE LEARNING PROJECT

The staff and administration at Kelly Bloomer's urban school saw transient students as disengaged not only from the school, but from the larger community. As a way of mending this rift, their students now complete a service learning project (SLP). The project requires students to:

- Identify a community problem. The students often identify problems relevant to teens, like gang violence and teen pregnancy.

- Create an action plan. Students outline what they will do to help with the problem.

These projects help engage students. When they investigate problems in the community, they feel more connected to the community. One twelfth-grade girl who'd gotten pregnant presented to the ninth-grade health classes. She told them about her typical day and the challenges of being a teen mom. When they study issues relevant to their lives, school becomes more relevant. Students who struggle with attendance can work on their SLP outside of school. The SLP even engages many of those students who once struggled with attendance. Transient kids are not integrated into your school community. They're an invisible underclass that arrives partway through the semester and leaves before final exams. These youngsters are disconnected, disengaged. An SLP effectively introduces the newcomers to their school and the larger community. An SLP can also help keep students who must be absent feel connected. To engage these challenged learners, projects *must* be relevant to students.

WHAT YOU CAN DO TOMORROW

- **Reach out to students with attendance problems.** A kind comment can really help a struggling kid. They might think you're angry at them for missing class. In fairness, some teachers do feel angry over absenteeism. Try, "I know you've struggled to come to school lately, but I'm here for you." Or, "Let's investigate ways to keep you on track even on days you miss."

- **Use technology.** The days when mom has to come to school to get her sick daughter's homework are gone. Online classroom platforms like Google Classroom make it possible for absent kids to stay at least partly, if not mostly, on track. If a learner is prone to missing time, develop an online relationship with that kid tomorrow. It could start with a simple email.

- **Negotiate student learning projects with struggling students.** Perhaps such a project could be a wonderful solution for a kid who struggles with attendance. Challenge the student to create a topic that will help the community but still be relevant to the curriculum.

- **Facilitate frequent interaction.** Be in communication with transient students frequently. They're accustomed to riding off into the sunset. Keep probing and checking. Ask permission to share what they've done with the rest of the class so that they're still contributing to and connecting with the other students.

Community service projects engage students in their schools and communities. Students with attendance problems can work on these projects outside of school, allowing them to complete their course objectives and maintain connections with the educational community.

HACK 32

ENGAGE AS YOU GRADE

THE PROBLEM: STUDENTS DON'T READ TEACHER COMMENTS

As a student, I was one of those kids. You know the type: My teacher would hand back my paper or project, having filled the margins with narratives written in red ink. These minor dissertations contained useful directives on how I could become a better student. But alas, these suggestions didn't engage me. All I wanted to know was my final grade. I didn't even consider reading the comments.

Yes, there must be such a thing as karma. Now I'm the teacher, and I know how supremely frustrating it is when students don't read my comments. Aside from feeling ignored, my concern is that these suggestions are wonderful opportunities for student growth that the kids are missing. Regardless, I struggled to get kids to read them.

THE HACK: ENGAGE STUDENTS BY GRADING WITH VERBAL FEEDBACK

Voice grading engages students because it allows a teacher to communicate so much more than written comments do. There's no tone or inflection in written comments. There's no laughter or warmth in written comments. Of course, there's the ALL CAPS RANT, but that seems more threatening than encouraging. The human voice can communicate encouragement so much more effectively than a written exhortation will.

> **Voice grading fosters dialogue between a student and teacher.**

Here are the basic steps to voice grading:

- Students submit an assignment electronically. A simple way to do this is through Google Docs.

- Teachers highlight a section of the student's submission and record comments.

- Students listen to the comments and then record replies. Students then make alterations.

Voice grading fosters dialogue between a student and teacher as students record responses to the feedback and teachers reply to them. Writing becomes more engaging, more collaborative—more of a process. There are many options for grading by voice, but I've had good results with Kaizena, an application that integrates nicely with Google Docs. You create class period sections and then Kaizena generates a student invite code. If you encounter difficulties, Kaizena has very responsive customer service.

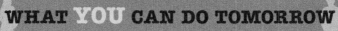
Shiva is known to be the only god who circumscribes all subjects of truth; beauty, wisdom and power (Willson 269). Shiva's dance hold the universe in balance, even though it is in constant dynamic motion. Shiva worshipers attend the celebration called Mahashivratri, where his idols are drenched in water, milk and honey, then worshipped (BBC Hinduism). The ritual is performed on the night of the same day Shiva danced the Tandav, it is said that the new moon appears and saves the world from ignorance and darkness (BBC Hinduism). Participants will stay awake all night while fasting and giving Shiva offerings of fruits and vegetables. Holy texts are sung and people in temples perform puja. Male and female characteristics of Shiva work simultaneously to manifest the universe, sometimes referred to as, the self who is fully absorbed in his own self (Williams 270). The saying "Shivam bhutva Shivam Yajet", translates to "meditate on Shiva to become like Shiva", and is held in high regard within Hindu culture, as Shiva's wisdom is greatly looked up to (Williams 270). Shiva is often misunderstood by his name, the destroyer, but in reality Shiva represents dissolution which is necessary for new aspects of life to form. This is crucial in completing the beautiful cycle of reincarnation. Shiva is often used as inspiration to Hindu's, temples are dedicated to Shiva and dot India's landscape, encouraging all to improve themselves further.

Image 32.1

WHAT YOU CAN DO TOMORROW

- **Add Kaizena to your Google Drive.** Once it's included, add classes and sections to your Kaizena homepage.
- **Direct students to join Kaizena.** Provide them with an invite code. The process is similar to inviting students to join Google Classroom.

- **Practice using voice feedback with a bell-ringer.** Entice them to write something short and simple. Coax an opinion or a prediction. Direct students to share with you what they've written electronically via email or Google Drive. Let the collaboration begin.

Voice feedback could revolutionize the way you perceive grading. If kids get accustomed to listening and responding to your comments, writing prompts will become collaborative, fostering engagement.

HACK 33

ROLL OUT THE READING ROLES

THE PROBLEM: MANY STUDENTS ARE REPULSED BY READING ASSIGNMENTS

WHEN I WAS in high school, I hated reading! My freshman year, we were forced to read *Great Expectations*. I remember absolutely nothing from that book. Our silent reading time was my "see what I can get away with" time. I was totally disengaged from the entire process. The book was irrelevant to my life—it wasn't, but it seemed that way to me. I earned (I use that term loosely) a D in the class. I needed more structure. I needed more concrete objectives. I needed the freedom to interact with my peers in constructive ways.

In contrast, I was once part of a small book club. We'd read, then convene to discuss. It was cool. As I read, I kept thinking about contributions I could make to our next meeting. A book club not only engages, it also turns reading into a fascinating opportunity to express and to bond with others.

When you read something interesting, you want to share it. When reading inspires you to embrace a new perspective, you want to express it. When reading motivates you to create something, you want to display it. Sharing, expressing, and displaying are foundational to successful book clubs, or what we will call them in this Hack, literature circles. Literature circles facilitate the wonderful social aspect of reading and sharing.

THE HACK: CREATE A LITERATURE CIRCLE FOR A READING ASSIGNMENT

Literature circles ramp up engagement, and they're not just for language arts. They should be used in any class where there's required reading. Student interaction in the literature circle can be open-ended or more guided, depending on your preferences and the needs of your students. Students who have more capacity to self-direct can read and hold discussion meetings with little instruction. However, if you believe your students need more structure, offer them reading roles. Some typical roles a teacher might assign are:

- Summarizer

- Discussion Director

- Connector

- Literary Luminary

- Illustrator

- Researcher

These roles accommodate various learning preferences. When the literature circles convene after the reading time, students share the work they've completed for each role.

My student, Olivia Wince, felt liberated by participating in a literature circle. Olivia is an artist, so she opted to take on the illustrator role. She was excited by the prospect of drawing a reading assignment:

> When I read something, I create a picture in my head. This helps me understand and remember. As I read through a text, I like to draw little doodles in the margins. The more complicated the subject, the more doodles I draw. Then, when I've completed the reading, I create a large picture inspired by my smaller drawings. This large drawing summarizes the main ideas of the reading.

Olivia read about Chinese philosophy in history class. She created the drawing in Image 33.1 to summarize and comprehend the reading.

Image 33.1

Not only did representing the reading via drawing help Olivia comprehend, it also helped other members of her literature circle: "I explained all the images, but what really helped was describing what I was going through as I drew. In other words, why I drew what I drew. The other students in the circle complimented me and said it helped them understand the complex ideas in the reading much better."

If you incorporate literature circles in your class, you may just find students borrowing tactics they used in the experience and applying them to readings in other subjects. Olivia certainly did: "I started drawing doodles for readings in my other classes, especially math and science."

WHAT YOU CAN DO TOMORROW

- **Research literature circles.** Plenty of internet resources offer information about this method. Search for "literature circle roles" or "conduct literature circles" to get instructions and resources.

- **Preview student roles for the literature circle.** Students can then volunteer to fulfill a role that appeals most to them.

- **Practice on a paragraph.** Before conducting a full-scale book read, have kids practice their roles by applying them to a paragraph and meeting to discuss it.

- **Arrange learners.** Make certain each group is well rounded with various learning preferences and perspectives represented.

- **Sponsor a short meet-and-greet.** Don't assume classmates know one another. Prompt them to do a brief icebreaker. This type of activity fosters relationships, which will facilitate a more productive and engaging literature circle.

- **Choose a compelling reading for the literature circle.** This is a wonderful opportunity to engage students in reading. A compelling reading could make this experience transformational.

Literature circles engage students in reading by connecting it to students' propensity to socialize. Such circles ramp up enjoyment and they facilitate comprehension regardless of the learning style, or perspective.

HACK 34

LET THEM BUILD IT

THE PROBLEM: STUDENTS HAVE NO IDEA HOW TO STUDY FOR A TEST

IN THE FALL of 1979, I was a freshman in college studying for my first political science exam. I had absolutely no idea what I was doing. I spread my notes and all the texts out in front of me, and just kept reading and rereading, over and over. It was all a blur. No patterns were emerging. I was lost. After hours of study and anxiety, I earned a 70 percent. Barely a C. I felt so totally demoralized that I thought of dropping out.

I'm not certain why I stayed, but I'm glad I did, because this experience taught me a lesson that helped me to find academic success. A week later, I had a history exam. I knew that my academic survival depended on a better performance, so I had to study differently. I'll give my younger self some credit. I kept thinking about some of the not-so-swift people I knew who had graduated from college: *If they can do it, certainly I can.* I knew I didn't need to study more—I had spent hours getting ready for the previous test. I needed to study smarter. And then I asked myself a life-altering question that seems so obvious and fundamental it's shocking that it took me eighteen years to figure it out (I was a late bloomer). I put myself in my professor's shoes and wondered, *What questions would I put on the test?*

When I considered the content through this lens, patterns emerged. I organized my study material and wrote potential prompt after potential prompt. I successfully anticipated the questions on that test and aced it. I never looked back.

THE HACK: CHALLENGE STUDENTS TO WRITE TEST QUESTIONS

Many students are like I was in 1979: aimless, anxious, and disengaged. They have no idea how to study. They're not asking themselves, *What will Mr. Sturtevant put on the test?* This hack will inject confidence in students and empower them to use a wonderful academic tool. I used to review the old-school way: pass out a review sheet, direct kids to complete it, ask if there were any questions, then implore them to study when they get home. That hardly qualifies as an engaging lesson. I wanted to commission learners to create outstanding assessments.

> **The more students try to create good test questions, the better they get at anticipating what the teacher would ask.**

Break students into small groups a couple of days prior to a unit test. Have each group organize the unit into subtopics. Each group member then will focus on one subtopic and formulate a number of potential questions associated with it. Each member will then share his or her speculations with the remainder of the group.

Once the students have questions for their sections completed, the next class will be ultra-engaging. Prompt each group: "What were your subtopics?" "What questions did you create with each subtopic?" Write some of the best prompts on the Smart Board and respond to student suggestions positively: "That's a wonderful question. Did any other groups come up with that one?"

The more you practice making up questions about content, the better the students will get at anticipating questions on assessments. Which brings me to the pay-off: Once your students get adept at creating thoughtful questions, they can actually write a majority of the test. You'll hear yourself saying, "I love that question so much, I'm putting it on the test!"

WHAT YOU CAN DO TOMORROW

- **Distribute assessment all-stars throughout the groups.** I take the top ten performers on the previous test and make them team captains. Small groups, no larger than three members, work best for this activity.

- **Randomly assign students to a team.** Just walk around the room counting kids off from 1 to 10. If you have some social pairings that must be avoided, this is a great way to avoid them. Your counting sequence is totally up to you.

- **Isolate groups and start the clock.** I often take students to the media center, or the gymnasium, or the cafeteria. I like big open spaces where groups can isolate themselves and focus. I give an exact window of time for them to be productive: "I'll give you exactly twenty-six minutes to complete your review." Limiting the timeframe focuses them quickly.

- **Divide and conquer.** Encourage learners to break the unit into sub-topics. Then, each group member focuses on a small, manageable sub-topic and creates potential test questions accordingly. Even advanced students who've already analyzed the unit content will benefit from helping their peers. (I helped a cute girl study for a test once in college. I couldn't get over how much better prepared I was by the process of helping her.)

- **Include outstanding student-created questions on the test.** The more students try to create good test questions, the better they get at anticipating what the teacher would ask. By year's end, students could be creating the entire test. Now, that's engagement.

To succeed on tests, students need to anticipate questions. Engage students in the test creation process by challenging them to create exam prompts.

TRANSFORM YOUR CLASS INTO A FOCUS GROUP

THE PROBLEM: TEACHERS ARE RELUCTANT TO ELICIT STUDENT FEEDBACK

NOLAN SAMPLES IS my current student teacher. He's a big dude—he played offensive line in college—but he has a calm demeanor and a sweet personality that puts students at ease. He connects with kids and engages them. What's really impressive, though, is the way he empowers students to help him become a better teacher. Nolan does this by asking kids a courageous and powerful question: "How'd I do?" I'm so impressed with his chutzpah that I'm determined to ask the same question once I'm back in the saddle. But I must confess, I'm a little nervous about it.

Nolan sees his actions as a way of amplifying student voice: "I started asking them how'd I do because I liked the idea of giving students a voice. I've learned from their input. I also believe this question engages students and helps build connections."

THE HACK: AFTER YOUR NEXT PRESENTATION, ASK STUDENTS HOW YOU DID

Treat your students as if they were a focus group to learn about the effectiveness of your instruction. You might be worried about students giving slacker advice like, "We should never be forced to take notes." You'll get some unhelpful suggestions, but the more you ask for input, the more helpful and specific the suggestions will become. Here's what Nolan has experienced: "I learned students wanted me to go slower and also be more direct and focused. The students pointed out that when I started, I gave them information overload. I really valued these lessons and I've become a better teacher as a result."

SurveyMonkey is a wonderful tool for obtaining anonymous student input via questionnaires. Periodically direct learners to join your focus group and help you become a more engaging teacher. Check out the four basic questions Nolan's example inspired in Image 35.1.

How Engaging was Today's Lesson?

1. Rate the pace of today's lesson...

2. Today's lesson's degree of difficulty was...

3. On a scale from 1-10, how engaged were you in today's lesson?

4. Make a suggestion to Mr. Sturtevant on how he can improve today's lesson.

Done

Image 35.1

WHAT YOU CAN DO TOMORROW

- **Create a simple focus group survey.** Four questions will suffice. You can repeat the same survey periodically—it'll be a great quantitative measure of growth in your ability to engage students.

- **Define focus groups for your class.** Many kids will be clueless about focus groups and their purpose. Explain what one is, why they're important, and how you hope to use the feedback to become a better teacher.

- **Ask your students to evaluate your lesson.** Students may be so shocked at your request that they have difficulty responding initially. You also may get some insincere feedback designed to reduce workload. But keep trying. Student contributions will improve dramatically with practice.

- **Embrace student input as constructive criticism.** Just remember, unlike the principal who evaluates you once a year, students watch you in action daily. They're potentially your greatest assets. Also remember that students can be wildly complimentary. Listen to student input, make some necessary adjustments, and prepare yourself for future glowing surveys.

Understand that students are your target audience, and ask them frequently, "How am I doing?" They're a wonderful source of information that can help you become a much more effective instructor.

HACK 36

OBSESS OVER GROUP DYNAMICS

THE PROBLEM: MANY STUDENT GROUPS ARE UNPRODUCTIVE

CONTEMPORARY EDUCATION PLACES a great deal of emphasis on collaboration. That's a good thing: Being a team player is a highly valued attribute. A high-functioning group that collaborates effectively is a wonderful impetus to engage. Teachers often group kids based on variables such as ability and skill sets. Such attributes are easily identifiable, but teachers simply must take compatibility into account as well. I teach ninth graders. Freshmen are hyper and dramatic. If you place the wrong kids together, the impact can make for pandemonium. Also, nothing frosts a motivated fifteen-year-old's gourd faster than having to do all the group's work to cover for slacker colleagues.

Samantha Bickley, a high-functioning freshman, has sometimes felt exploited by fellow group members. Here's what she says about frustrating group scenarios: "I hate it when I have to take over and do other people's jobs because they're screwing around."

Samantha has some wonderful advice for educators: "Teachers should take into account skills. That way, the project can get done more efficiently. But teachers also need to know each group member's personality, so they know who's going to accomplish what and they can anticipate and then deal with problems."

THE HACK: CREATE INTERACTIVE, SUPPORTIVE, AND PRODUCTIVE GROUPS

If you're a little stumped on how to create effective and engaging groups, check out the article "10 Recommendations for Improving Group Work" by Maryellen Weimer on the blog *Faculty Focus*. I particularly like two of her recommendations:

- Consider roles for group members,

- Require individual members to keep track of their contributions.

Collaborating in high-functioning groups can be most engaging for students.

A great tactic is to allow students to organize themselves based on role preference. Much like formal roles in a literature circle, they could choose one of the following:

- Illustrator

- Connector

- Summarizer

- Researcher

You'll probably have to even things out. You might have to convince someone who wants to draw that the group desperately needs a summarizer. Once kids assume various roles, you can match the right illustrator with the perfect researcher to maximize social harmony and foster productivity.

It's also helpful to have students document their own progress. You might use a productivity log or empower them to apply the project rubric to their efforts.

WHAT YOU CAN DO TOMORROW

- **Make your objective clear.** Explain that your goal is to help all students function better in groups. Clarifying your objective allows students to focus on what's most important. Try a statement along these lines: "Today, we're going to do a group dynamics and productivity exercise. This activity should help us be successful on the project we're going to start tomorrow."

- **Disperse the leaders.** Let's say you have a class of twenty-five and you want five groups of five. Direct students to elect five can-do kids who will act as group leaders and project managers. Randomly assign project managers a number from one to five.

- **Conduct some social engineering.** Disperse the drama. Students can think you're randomly assigning the remaining students to groups one through five, but actually you're separating the drama-driven and assigning them to well-suited project leaders.

- **Construct a group mission statement.** Challenge each group to create a role for each member. You may need to interact and make suggestions for appropriate roles. Make it clear that group members must take on jobs they're willing to do.

- **Have each group member offer an obstacle the group might encounter.** This may foster some fascinating dialogue as students negotiate regarding potential problems. Be prepared to jump in and mediate. The project manager then creates a group mission statement, which includes a list of the job(s) each member pledged to do and an overall objective.

- **Require individual members to keep track of their contributions.** Craft a simple self-evaluation rubric for each group member. This will introduce a level of accountability that should help slacker group members focus and make others confident that their work will be judged appropriately.

Collaborating in high-functioning groups can be most engaging for students. Select group membership carefully, and add structure and accountability when necessary.

LET YOUR FREAK FLAG FLY

THE PROBLEM: TEACHERS OFTEN TRY TO SUBMERGE THEIR ECCENTRICITIES INSTEAD OF CELEBRATING THEM

OUR STUDENTS HAVE us down cold. They can imitate us at lunch, they notice when we experiment with a new hair style, they immediately recognize our new eyeglass frames, they evaluate our fashion choices, they sense our moods, they know if we've been working out, and they can tell when we're in need of a good night's sleep. We're under their microscope.

THE HACK: DISCOVER YOUR INTERESTING PECULIARITIES

A few years back, Charlie Rowley became my student teacher. Charlie is good-looking, friendly, and calm. When Charlie strolled into my class on the first day, all buffed up and square-jawed, my girls immediately perked up. I'm certain they were thinking, *Whoa. This is a massive upgrade from Mr. Sturtevant.* The athletes in the class seemed drawn to Charlie too, perhaps because he had been a college football player. But there were a handful of kids, not more than five, but that's a significant minority, whose body language told a much less welcoming story. Their demeanor proclaimed, "Oh great. They sent us another jock social studies teacher."

I pulled Charlie aside and explained this delicate social dynamic. Charlie didn't hesitate. "Okay. Let's see if I can win them over. This sounds like fun." He's a great guy.

Over the next few weeks, Charlie shelved his ego and worked hard to engage his reluctant contingent. It was working. They started warming up to him. And then one day, one of Charlie's emerging converts made an amazing observation. Here's how Charlie describes it:

> Out of the blue, a student pointed out how often I say the word "solid." I didn't even realize I said it so much 'til I started thinking about it. When this kid pointed it out, the other students laughed in agreement. Kids started calling out "solid" to me in the hallway. This stupid phrase brought us together and helped me engage all my students. Also, I'm a pretty calm guy, but I found saying "solid" energized me, which helped with engagement too. I started stepping toward students and pointing at them when they did something solid. I'd step, point, and say, *"That's solid."*

Like Charlie, who was initially clueless about his use of the word "solid," or the amazing potential of this tendency, you probably also have interesting behavioral tics that will aid in student engagement. If you're unsure what your interesting proclivities are, ask your students. They'll tell you.

WHAT YOU CAN DO TOMORROW

- **Prime the pump.** Direct students to list some of their odd tendencies or quirks. This prompt can inspire some interesting conversation.

- **Prime the pump some more.** Direct students to list some odd tendencies or quirks of friends and family. For example, I got stung by a bee the other day. My wife told a friend, "Jim got bit by a bee." I have never been able to figure out why she says that bees bite people. It's weird, but I guess it's part of her charm.

- **Insert yourself into the fray.** Ask students a simple question: "Is there anything I do or say on a regular basis that you guys think is strange or unique?" You may be totally shocked by their responses. Also, their responses may come later, down the road, when you point at a student with your foot while performing a perfect Radio City Rockettes kick.

> • **Exploit your interesting eccentricities to engage students.** If you do something odd, own it, exploit it, and find ways to perform it on a regular basis.

Discover your unique quirks. Exploit these behavioral fingerprints as potential engagement tools.

ASSESS YOUR ASSESSMENTS

THE PROBLEM: MANY TESTS DO A POOR JOB OF ASSESSING LEARNING

Picture this: You're having a medical procedure done. Before they put you under, you tell the doctor, "I want you to perform this procedure from memory. You're absolutely not permitted to use any resources. You may not look at your phone, consult the Internet, and you're especially not allowed to ask other doctors for help. If you don't complete the procedure within an hour, you must put down your instruments and exit the operating room."

It would be hard to imagine many patients surviving such a setup. And yet, that's pretty much what teachers do to kids daily. No wonder many students suffer from test anxiety. Furthermore, many tests merely measure short-term memory. I doubt that your students would do very well if they had to retake last semester's final exams.

Disengaged kids do poorly on tests and often suffer from test anxiety. Let's try to bring them back into the fold.

THE HACK: ALLOW STUDENTS TO DEMONSTRATE WHAT THEY'VE LEARNED IN A COLLABORATIVE FASHION

Michael Dunlea, a fabulous second-grade teacher from the beautiful state of New Jersey, inspired me to change the way I assess by assigning his students to make paper airplanes: "I challenged my students to design a test to see who made the best plane. It turned into a very cool conversation with lots of give and take." Michael's students designed something similar to a long jump competition to see which plane would fly the farthest. One of the little guys beautifully demonstrated the limitations

Use any assessment to begin a conversation.

of the student-created assessment, which looked a lot like most academic tests with a clearly visible grading scale and winners and losers. "I asked him, 'Don't you think you made a good plane?' He responded, 'I flew it all the way across the room, but then during the competition I choked.'" This statement about choking led to wonderful give-and-take between Michael and his students. He empowered them to create a better assessment.

Michael's beautiful story reminded me of the typical test anxiety students frequently describe: *I studied! I knew the material! I just went blank when I got the test!* The fact that he allowed his second graders to create their own assessment inspired me to alter my students' assessment as they wrapped up their study of the Israeli-Palestinian conflict. I simply told them, "Come up with a solution to the conflict, then demonstrate it." Two students did just that. Please watch their persuasive mini-documentary, which you can find via Image 38.1.

This video was just the beginning of a wonderful conversation between these young women and me. As I watched their video I jotted down these questions:

- Was this the best title for your documentary?

- Which side would be most opposed to your solution?

- How would you overcome this opposition?

- What role does terrorism play in this conflict?

- Why are the occupied territories significant?

- Your solution is perfectly logical. Why hasn't it materialized?

Image 38.1

I presented the girls with these questions in the form of comments on their blogs. This gave them time to think before we met. When we did get together, a fascinating conversation ensued. I was thrilled when they decided their video could have been better and told me how they'll improve the next one. Their documentary was merely an initial step toward deep investigation of an important topic.

WHAT YOU CAN DO TOMORROW:

- **Create an essential questions handout for the material you're assessing.** These questions will act as a launch pad for self-directed student engagement.

- **Challenge students to demonstrate deep understanding.** Tell students that you're releasing them to learn in their own way. You may have to offer suggestions for the form assessments might take, like a video, a podcast, an artifact, or a demonstration, but also allow space for creativity. Make certain they understand that they must address the essential questions.

- **Offer the opportunity for either collaboration or independent effort.** But use professional judgment on this front. Some students are productive in groups, some are not. Some kids hide in groups. Account for these variables.

- **Use any assessment to begin a conversation.** As you are assessing a product, create a script of questions you can pose to students which will inspire them to go deeper.

Engage students by making self-directed, engaging assessments that allow students to demonstrate what they know. Profound collaboration begins after the assessment.

HACK 39

TRADE BLAH, BLAH, BLAH FOR ZEN

THE PROBLEM: YOUR STUDENTS ZONE OUT WHEN YOU PRESENT TO THEM

I'LL BET YOU'VE watched a classic Charlie Brown cartoon and heard a teacher's voice droning, "Wah-wah-wah." These unintelligible robotic sounds communicate the effect a teacher's voice often has on students. Charlie and his classmates are totally disengaged, but that doesn't stop the teacher. This scene resonates with viewers because most have experienced this painful phenomenon.

I remembered Charlie Brown's teacher recently while reading *Presentation Zen* by Garr Reynolds. This book teaches presenters how to avoid giving the droning, Charlie Brown-teacher presentations that we all dread. Reynolds's book stirred my deep and profound affirmation. I had not been able to verbalize or formulate my ideas until I read its illuminating views on what constitutes a compelling presentation. After I finished the book I took decisive action, which fundamentally improved they way I interact with my students.

THE HACK: TRANSFORM A PRESENTATION USING
THE *PRESENTATION ZEN* METHOD

This book knocked me off my perch. It challenged everything I thought I knew about presentation. Here are some DOs and DON'Ts:

DON'T:

- Include bullet points

- Insert animations or particularly flashy transitions

- Create text-heavy slides

- Use distracting backgrounds

- Clutter slides with multiple images

- Read while presenting, particularly with bullet points

DO:

- Focus each slide with one compelling image

- Limit text to a title or phrase

- Enchant the audience with stories that the image supports or inspires

- Provide the audience with a leave-behind that includes important information

Image 39.1

Reynolds's recommendations made perfect sense. I've attended awful lectures where the presenter read bullet points off a PowerPoint slide. Haven't you? I tried in vain to multitask, to listen to the presenter and read the slide simultaneously. After reading this book, I vowed to fundamentally alter the way I deliver content. It's worked, and my students are incredibly complimentary.

I go into more detail about the potential of presenting to students in this fashion in the episode of the *Hacking Engagement* podcast that you'll find via Image 39.1.

If you'd like to see an example of a power image with bold but sparse text, look at Image 39.2.

FLIPPED INSTRUCTION

Image 39.2

My flipped lecture on India will serve as an example of the power of a good presentation. This presentation is stocked with beautiful public domain images easily found with basic web searches. The images gave me a platform to launch into compelling narratives—they cry out for an explanation, a story. It intrigues students in the opening days of the semester when I introduce flipped presentations. They did a wonderful job of extracting information from it. Follow the QR code in Image 39.3 if you're inclined to watch.

image 39.3

WHAT YOU CAN DO TOMORROW

- **Visit presentationzen.com.** I've provided the bare basics in the Hack section. Reynolds explains exactly why such presentations are superior and goes into the specifics of how to create a beautiful, compelling, and impactful one.

- **Alter one of your presentations using Reynolds's ideas.** It could be a flipped lecture or a presentation you deliver in class. It could be a PowerPoint, a Prezi, or whatever platform you prefer.

- **Conduct a public domain image search.** Be a good role model and use public domain images in your presentations. Find awesome images that will inspire compelling narratives.

- **Create a leave-behind.** Here's where you can include your treasured bullet points. Pass out the handout at the conclusion of your presentation. This timing is crucial if you want the bullet points to have impact.

- **Debrief your students.** Ask for feedback. Ask how you can improve.

Students see so many ineffective presentations that they almost automatically disengage when the lights go down. The ideas promoted in *Presentation Zen* could revolutionize your classroom. Tell compelling stories about inspiring images.

HACK 40

BE MORE LIKE HOCKING COLLEGE

THE PROBLEM: DIRECT INSTRUCTION ALIENATES SOME STUDENTS

DAVID IS A bright and creative twenty-three-year-old. His elementary, middle school, and high school teachers all talked about his potential, but potential doesn't equal results, and David's grades at those levels languished. He wasn't engaged: "I would sit in bland classrooms and I wouldn't feel any connection to what I was learning. Whatever the subject, we were expected to fully understand something, but rarely did we do what it was we were supposed to be learning."

Things didn't get better for David when he graduated from high school. He went to a large public university. In order to fulfill freshman requirements, he was thrown into basic education classes. He felt the same disconnect he had in high school and now his classes were huge. Not only did he feel disengaged from the direct instruction method and the subject, but also from the instructor. After just one semester, he concluded that college wasn't worth the price and dropped out.

For three years, David did what many college dropouts do—he worked odd jobs, socialized with friends, and just barely afforded the rent. But there was a deep yearning in him to do something meaningful and engaging. He decided to enroll in the ecotourism program at Hocking College in Nelsonville, Ohio. Hocking offers associates degrees in over fifty majors and does what vocational and technical schools have always done best: provide hands-on learning.

THE HACK: ENGAGE YOUR STUDENTS BY HAVING THEM *DO* YOUR SUBJECT

David achieved the dean's list his first semester at Hocking. He describes the eco-tourism program as hands-on:

> For every hour of lecture we have three to four hours of lab. We learn the process, then do the process. Much of my lab time is spent in the beautiful rolling Wayne National Forest. Sometimes I struggle in lectures, but then we go outside and everything becomes clear. I learned at Hocking that I have a real interest and talent in forestry. I'm engaged at Hocking.

Schools at all levels, including liberal arts colleges, are embracing the hands-on example set by institutions like Hocking. Apply the ratio of three applications to one instruction in your class. Turn a healthy portion of your class into a lab:

- History students can investigate original sources and create museum exhibits.

- Math students can design structures or calculate the probability of candidates winning the next election.

- Science students can evaluate the water quality in a nearby stream.

- English students can read poetry to elderly shut-ins.

- Psychology students can create advertising campaigns for their favorite snacks.

Constantly ask yourself, *How can my students apply their knowledge for the next topic?* By devoting the majority of class time to your students doing instead of sitting and listening, you just might engage a great kid like David. This would be a wonderful thing, and I can speak from experience. David Sturtevant just happens to be my son.

WHAT YOU CAN DO TOMORROW

- **Identify an activity.** Analyze tomorrow's lesson. Make a list of potential activities embedded in the lesson.

- **Turn your class into a lab.** Apply the Hocking three-to-one template to tomorrow's lesson. If your class is 48 minutes long, instruct for 12 minutes and then conduct a lab for 36.

- **Create a lab where students do the lesson.** Create a challenge that will engage kids like David. If you're stumped, solicit colleagues, search Google, or search *Lesson Planet* for ideas.

- **Get your students out of the classroom.** It could be as simple as going to the gym, the atrium, the cafeteria, the football field, the parking lot, or the stairwell. Perhaps these excursions could eventually venture off campus.

Direct instruction can be almost painful for some kids. Get students out of their seats and doing. Engage students by creating learning laboratories.

HACK 41

GATHER STUDENTS AROUND THE FIRE

THE PROBLEM: MANY STUDENT PRESENTATIONS ARE ROBOTIC

APRIL DOMINE, MY former superintendent, once made a powerful suggestion. She encouraged me to read Daniel Pink's *A Whole New Mind*. It was an amazing recommendation. The crux of the book is that the right side of the brain is going to be the star of the future. The subtitle indicates its focus: *Moving from the Information Age to the Conceptual Age.* As I read this excellent book, I felt Pink was verbalizing everything I've always felt about the learning process. And to top it off, he is a fellow Buckeye.

Pink devotes an entire chapter to the power of the story. In it, he challenges the reader to recall an important data point from one of the opening chapters. No doubt most of the readers struggle to recall the specific statistic—I certainly did. To contrast with this example of retrieving a memory, he then asks readers to recall a fascinating comparison between the legendary John Henry, the "steel driving man" who could not work as fast as a steel powered hammer, and Gary Kasperov, the chess champion defeated by the IBM computer in 1997. Both John Henry and Gary Kasperov demonstrated the limitations of even the most skilled and determined human in the face of advancing technology.

When Pink referred to these rich narratives, the feelings I had when I first read them, their lessons, and many of the details immediately surfaced. Storytelling is a powerful tool that's underused. Not only do teachers need to tell more stories, but so do students.

THE HACK: COMMISSION STUDENTS TO ENGAGE CLASSMATES WITH STORIES

Many presentations leave their victims comatose. Challenge your students to harness the power of a great story. Enliven student presentations with the simple but profound power of storytelling.

Unleash student creativity by allowing them to be the storytellers.

Familiarize students with the elements of a good story. Brian Klems has a wonderful piece in *Writer's Digest*, "The 5 Essential Story Ingredients," which can be found with a simple search at WritersDigest.com. Have students read this piece or research elements of a good story. Then, agree as a class on five elements and challenge kids to use those elements as a template for their stories. Take whatever topic you'd like your class to work on and challenge students to bring it to life by the virtual campfire.

On story day, break students into small groups, darken your room for impact, have your young campers activate the campfire apps on phones or Chromebooks, and then let them animate your lesson.

WHAT YOU CAN DO TOMORROW

- **Designate a topic in your curriculum that's ripe for peer teaching.** Topics that include personal narratives are powerful. I had students retell the story of the great Indian king Ashoka from a personal perspective.

- **Build around the five essential story ingredients.** These elements will be the story template. Even with the template, some kids will moan about writer's block. Just be cool and patient. You may have to pair some students to get it done. You also might want to include a time limit, as some kids are a little long-winded.

- **Create a campfire.** As a kid, I loved being regaled by a campfire or beside a snapping fireplace. In order for student stories to have oomph and ambiance, direct them to search "Virtual Fireplace" on YouTube. When it's story time and they're in their small groups, have them display this virtual fire on their Chromebooks or phones while you turn down the lights.

- **Select group membership wisely.** As with any social gathering, if you mix the wrong guests at a table, the result can range from abject boredom to armed conflict.

Stories are an awesome way to engage students. Unleash student creativity by allowing them to be the storytellers.

HACK 42

CORRAL THE WORD "LIKE"

THE PROBLEM: SOME TEACHERS SEEM DISTANT AND UNAPPROACHABLE

I VIVIDLY REMEMBER BEING seven years old and hooking my glove on the end of my bat, throwing it over my shoulder, smooshing my baseball cap on my head, and walking to baseball practice through my hilly little hometown of New Concord, Ohio. It was a Saturday, a warm sunny spring day. My teacher's house was en route to the ball field. Heck yes, I had a crush on Mrs. B. What I didn't anticipate was that when I turned the corner to pass her house, she'd be doing yardwork in capri stretch pants. It took my breath away.

You see, in 1968, female teachers wore dresses to school. We thought they dressed like that all the time. But here was Mrs. B, looking like a normal 30-something 1960s mom. Seeing her like that was obviously thrilling, but more important, it humanized her. She saw me, waved and yelled over, "Hey, Jimmy! Get a hit for me today." I gave her a big smile and waved back. This tender, innocent experience taught me a lot about engaging kids. Sometimes, they have to see you as an actual human being.

THE HACK: DEPUTIZE YOUR STUDENTS TO HELP
YOU BREAK AN ANNOYING HABIT

Confess to your class that you have a habit you'd like to break. Of course, you don't want to expose your kids to a gambling problem or alcoholism. I'd even steer clear of talking about quitting a cigarette habit. Instead, let your students help you master a more innocent annoying tendency. It will humanize you, make you seem less stuffy. My current self-improvement project is to reduce my use of the word "like." Obviously, it's fine to use when you're comparing things, but I use it too much as ridiculous filler. My fifteen-year-old female students spout "like" as frequently as they utter proper nouns. Conversations in my room quickly turn into like-fests. With respect to overusing the word, my students are not good role models!

Over the past few weeks, I've had students call me out when I use "like" as a filler. We've had a blast. They're certainly engaged in this little game. They're pretty aggressive and unforgiving, but I've dramatically reduced the number of "likes" I blab and my students have even become conscious of how often they say it. This silly little exercise has engaged my students, made me seem more human and approachable, and brought us closer together as a class.

WHAT YOU CAN DO TOMORROW

- **Identify an innocent personal habit or tendency.** One year I had my students help me with my posture. I had student volunteers demonstrate good posture and bad. My kids loved crabbing at me if I slouched. If you can't come up with an idea, ask your students. You may overuse a word, chew your nails, or rock back and forth when you speak. You may be totally unaware of annoying tendencies.

- **Announce your goal to students.** Indicate that you need their help and deputize them to help police your habit.

- **Challenge students to confess an annoying habit they'd like to eliminate.** You'll have a few volunteers. You can all go through detox together.

It's important your students see you as an actual human being. Empowering them to help you with an annoying habit will be an engaging bonding experience.

SURROUND YOURSELF WITH ANCIENT GREEKS

THE PROBLEM: STUDENTS ARE OFTEN INTIMIDATED BY COMPLEX CONCEPTS

SOCRATES UNDERSTOOD FORMATIVE assessment 2,500 years ago. His student would make an assertion and then the Great One would start probing. Much like an annoying three-year-old, he'd keep asking questions and follow-ups. Socrates' good-natured interrogations would cause students to bob and weave, refine and alter. Eventually, the young Athenian student would strike bedrock. In the process of finding that firm foundation, this ancient adolescent would demonstrate a solid and evolving understanding of the concept. The student might still disagree with classmates, and Socrates for that matter, but those disagreements would be based on reason.

Unfortunately, when it comes to discussing complex ideas in modern classrooms, many students keep a low profile, being totally disengaged or profoundly intimidated. In order to bring such students out of the weeds and into the intellectual light of day, copy the Great One and conduct a Socratic Circle.

THE HACK: CONDUCT A SOCRATIC CIRCLE

Socratic Circles are not debates. Sure, disagreements may occur in the process of discussing ideas, but generally the focus is on helping one another understand a complex issue or topic. Understanding materializes when students question one another. The discussion format requires disengaged students to participate, even

Socratic Circles are an engaging way to help all students grasp complex ideas.

if it's to ask a two- or three-word question, like *What is karma?* Those loaded questions play a crucial role. They foster deeper understanding and participation, regardless of how engaged and advanced students are, as they struggle to respond, clarify, and explain. It's truly magical.

The teacher remains silent outside the circle and allows students to Socratize one another. This distance is crucial, and difficult for many instructors. If there's a period of awkward silence, teachers, just be cool. You can throw out a prompt to get the conversation rolling, but make it brief, then detach. Embrace the mantra *Silence is Golden*.

For an outstanding resource, check out Matt Copeland's book *Socratic Circles*. Copeland provides the nuts and bolts on how to create an epic circle. Image 43.1 takes you to a blog post, in which I provide additional detail about how I've applied and tailored Copeland's methods.

Image 43.1

Here are crucial elements to fostering an engaging Socratic Circle:

1. Push half the desks into the center to form a tight circle. This will create an intimate setting. The outer circle can sit on the other desks and lord over their subjects.

2. Divide the class into two groups. One circle sits on the outside and silently evaluates the performance of the inner circle. After the inner circle has concluded their discussion, the outer circle offers feedback on their performance. Then the roles are switched.

3. Give each circle about ten minutes to pontificate. If the conversation is rolling, by all means let it go a little longer, but make sure to give the other circle a chance to move into the center.

4. Make certain each circle has some extroverts.

5. Create an entrance ticket. Have the students demonstrate they've prepared for the Socratic Circle.

6. Create an exit ticket. This is a great assessment tool.

WHAT YOU CAN DO TOMORROW

- **Identify an upcoming, meaty, complex topic for a Socratic Circle.** Which topics did students struggle with last semester? Which topics have the potential to elicit engaging conversation?

- **Create a number of thought-provoking prompts and provide them to the students prior to the discussion.** Awesome questions fuel the Socratic Circle. Even with the most provocative of questions, though, the teacher will need to prime the pump initially.

- **Intervene only when absolutely necessary.** In Socratic Circles the teacher says very little, leaving the onus on the students to keep the conversation going. In the most successful of discussions, the teacher would not be able to participate because it's hard to get a word in edgewise.

Socratic Circles are an engaging way to help all students grasp complex ideas. They also constitute a wonderful informal way to measure student understanding of complex topics.

SHOW-AND-TELL 2.0: *THE OPEN MIC*

THE PROBLEM: THE CLASSROOM INTERACTIONS
TEND TO BE ONE-DIMENSIONAL

JENNIFER GONZALEZ HAS taught at both the middle school and college levels. Now, in addition to being a full-time mom, Jennifer is an author, a podcast host extraordinaire, and a blogger. If you want fresh ideas on education, please check out her website, cultofpedagogy.com, and subscribe to her wonderful *Cult of Pedagogy* program on iTunes.

When I asked Jennifer about engagement, I figured she'd offer some high-tech contraption or exotic electronic technique. But while she loves those resources, she's also all about relationships:

> Our students have hidden talents. In my English class, I encouraged kids to perform for their peers. We called it *The Open Mic*. I was amazed at how these performances profoundly impacted my class. I've tried this at different schools, in different states, with diverse students, and it worked the same. It created an amazing communal feeling—not a school spirit thing, a *this is our class* thing. These were tight and intimate experiences. Music helps you see a kid in a different light, performances make kids proud of one another. I just wished I would've done it earlier in the semester.

THE HACK: CREATE *THE OPEN MIC* DAY IN YOUR CLASS

You might be thinking *It takes a lot of guts to get up in front of peers and sing.* Agreed. But kids can do all kinds of things during *The Open Mic*; it's not just about singing. They can:

- Play an instrument

- Recite a poem

- Perform a magic trick

- Demonstrate flexibility

- Do a live sketch, portrait, or caricature

- Display their photography

- Show their YouTube video

- Describe their favorite cookie recipe and provide samples (yes, the teacher gets one)

- Display and describe their painting, pottery, or woodworking

- Show their skateboarding video

- Demonstrate they can sneeze with their eyes open (yes, it's possible—I've done it)

Image 44.1

> **Create a family-like atmosphere in your class by allowing students to express themselves to supportive and fascinated peers.**

Jennifer suggests cajoling a few extroverted kids to volunteer for the maiden voyage to loosen up the class. Maybe the last day of every grading period could be devoted to *The Open Mic*.

The final caveat is audience preparation. Jennifer explains: "Performing in front of peers entails such an element of risk. I did a lot of audience prep, bordering on threats, about how supportive they had to be. But it's worth the risk because there's huge potential payoff. It helped create an outstanding family-like atmosphere in my class. When kids feel they belong, engagement spikes." Follow QR code 44.1 to the *Hacking Engagement* podcast to listen to my lively conversation with Jennifer Gonzalez about *The Open Mic*.

WHAT YOU CAN DO TOMORROW

- **Approach an outgoing kid about the idea.** Perhaps this youngster could sing or play the guitar. Even if she is not willing, she'll probably point you to someone who is.

- **Prompt students with an anonymous survey.** Give students a slip of paper. Have them write their names on the blank side, then flip it over and respond to the prompt: "What would you be willing to demonstrate, perform, or display for your peers?" You may get some blank sheets back. Don't fret about this for a second. There should be *zero* pressure on any student to perform.

- **Turn it into a guessing game.** See if students can guess who wrote *I can juggle*, or *I can demonstrate an extreme yoga posture*. Peers might guess immediately, or be shocked by what they learn. Regardless, this little match game just may give reluctant students the subtle push they need to step up to the mic.

- **Promote *The Open Mic.*** Explain to students your goal of creating a supportive, collaborative class. Indicate what day *The Open Mic* will be and encourage them to participate.

Create a family-like atmosphere in your class by allowing students to express themselves to supportive and fascinated peers.

MANDATE
MERITOCRACY MONDAYS

THE PROBLEM: CLASS PARTICIPATION ON MONDAY IS NONEXISTENT

COMMUNISM IS NOT productive. I've taught this in many different social studies classes over several decades. There's just not enough incentive. Capitalism, on the other hand, gets it: *The profit incentive is ultra-motivating.* Please apply capitalist wisdom to your classroom. You might be thinking, *Students get a final grade—isn't that incentive enough?* Perhaps, but many kids enjoy a good, solid, friendly, and low-risk competition with their peers, especially if there's a reward for the victor. This is the dynamic behind *Meritocracy Mondays.*

Interestingly enough, if you're successful with transforming your Mondays, you'll find student engagement improves the rest of the week. Many students have no experience with participating. Slowly and tentatively starting to take part on Mondays removes the novelty. Participation in the future, regardless of whether it's immediately rewarded, will be more likely.

THE HACK: INSTITUTE *MERITOCRACY MONDAYS*

You can reward students for many things: effort, good citizenship, kindness, enthusiasm, or interesting analysis. It's entirely up to you. Some days I reward a student just because they seem to need it. In my class, Monday is the day when students get an incentive boost. Your reward day does not have to be a Monday, but give it a cool label:

- Talented Tuesdays

- Winning Wednesdays

- Thoughtful Thursdays

- Frisky Fridays

After you've decided which day needs the adrenaline rush, throw in some unbridled capitalism by rewarding students for participation. These rewards don't have to be academic or expensive. I like to reward students in various ways:

- Restroom passes that can be used during the non-instructional portions of class

- A chance to eliminate one question from the next assignment

- Any type of food that's available

- Gofer for the day—the winner gets to do any needed errands on a designated day

- A bonus point

- Or, my favorite, a heart-felt compliment

Incentives such as these engage students, and they're low risk. It's rarely controversial if a student is rewarded with a restroom pass. Also, consider a cool way to reward. When I'm awarding bonus points, I use an invented sweeping sign language routine, which I demonstrate in Images 45.1 and 45.2.

Image 45.1   Image 45.2

You could create artifacts for any of the rewards:

- Nontransferable tickets to the restroom

- A laminated *Gofer for the Day* license plate

- A coupon that authorizes the student to eliminate one test question

WHAT YOU CAN DO TOMORROW

- **Create cool titles for Monday through Friday.** As silly as it may seem, putting a title on the day makes it special.

- **Compose a list of reward options**. Think about what rewards will appeal to your particular students.

- **Complete a *Bonus Day Bonanza* survey.** Part one will give students choice on which day of the week will be the bonus day. Part two will prompt them to select which reward option will be distributed that week. Students can change options each week or stick with a favorite. Perhaps those rewarded could select from the menu.

- **Share the results**. After all surveys have been completed, show kids how they voted. Perhaps an interesting class discussion will ensue.

- **Plan games.** Think about strategic, reward-worthy prompts you can sprinkle into your presentation on bonus day. With experience, awesome prompts will start emerging organically.

Create your own version of *Meritocracy Mondays* to engage students. Incentivize class participation to raise interest and energy in your class.

HACK 46

ENTICE STUDENTS TO DO HILL SPRINTS

THE PROBLEM: STUDENTS RESIST TAKING NOTES

My body is like a Honda Civic, only instead of oil changes, it's subjected to a biweekly workout that's truly awful. There's a steep hill (one of the few in Central Ohio) by my house. It's man-made and part of the Alum State Park Dam. It's an 80-yard incline. Twice a week, I sprint this hill ten times. In my youth, I could pick 'em up and lay 'em down. Now, as an older man, I'm much slower, but the burn feels identical to my high school track and field days. I don't like doing this workout. Doing reps 8, 9, and 10 are like entering the Gates of Hell. While I dislike the process, I love what hill running does for my body. And when I'm running that hill, I'm ultra-engaged.

I require my students to master note taking. Some probably consider it similar to doing reps 8, 9, and 10 of my workout. But even the ones who complain benefit significantly. I've had more than one student thank me for instilling this skill. As with my dislike for running the hill, students can benefit from things they don't necessarily enjoy.

THE HACK: CHALLENGE STUDENTS TO MASTER CORNELL NOTES

When I entered college, I had no idea how to take notes. I was like a court stenographer. I'd write down everything the prof said with virtually no understanding. I don't want my students to suffer my fate. Cornell-style notes give students direction and a template. Cornell notes inspire students to determine essential questions, anticipate test questions, organize their ideas, chunk material into main ideas, summarize complete presentations, and record ideas they find confusing. Students continually evaluate the material in the process of organizing and evaluation. It's what the Cornell notes people refer to fondly as repetitions.

If you flip your presentations like I do, Cornell notes make a wonderful assessment and accountability tool. You can assess:

- Engagement with the flipped presentation

- Thoroughness in the note taking

- Analysis in designating essential questions and essential concepts

- Effectiveness at anticipating potential test questions

- Reflective creation of clarifying questions

This system will engage and empower your students, but they may not enjoy it as much as they do some of the other hacks.

WHAT YOU CAN DO TOMORROW

- **Show students a Cornell notes tutorial video.** If you search for Cornell notes online, you'll find plenty of tutorials. I like the AVID Cornell notes video. It's thirteen minutes long and quite engaging. It gives students direction and also explains why the Cornell note taking system is so effective. But if AVID's video isn't available, there are plenty of options.

- **Have students complete a Cornell notes template as they watch the tutorial.** There are plenty of templates available online. You can even use a Google Form Cornell notes template so students can share their efforts with you electronically. Have students complete the template as they watch a tutorial video.

- **Designate a flipped presentation for your maiden Cornell notes voyage.** Students will complete the template outside of class. You'll then evaluate their level of engagement on the flipped lesson based on their performance on the Cornell template.

Some engaging classroom activities are very important, but not necessarily joyful. Cornell notes offer an efficient way for students to engage with a presentation.

HACK 47

PEERLESS PEER TEACHING WITH THE VOWEL SQUAD

THE PROBLEM: YOUR KIDS CAN'T SIT STILL

SARA SAWDEY IS a teaching prodigy. This student teacher from Muskingum University *gets* engagement. She has a knack for engaging seven-year-old boys who would rather be in the gym playing dodge ball instead of sitting in class learning to read and write. Can you even remotely fathom how hard sitting all day must be for Sara's first graders? I can relate. Even my high schoolers would love to be running, skating, jumping, dancing, shooting hoops, or bench pressing rather than sitting at a desk. Please remember, your students do a great deal of sitting. It's unnatural to sit for that much of the day; it's unhealthy.

THE HACK: EMPLOY PEER TEACHING GROUPS

Sara does a masterful job of empowering kids to acquire deep understanding and then engage their classmates:

> I had an intervention group of eight rowdy boys who had to learn the vowel sounds. These kids could not focus sitting at their desks. They were obsessed with moving. So I took them to the gymnasium. Each boy had a school-issued iPad. I challenged them to produce an iMovie about the vowel sounds that we could show to their classmates. They embraced this responsibility. But I wasn't interested in an ordinary standing-and-talking video, I wanted them to teach

through movement. I wanted them to use all parts of their bodies. This whole-brained approach to learning and peer teaching builds neuron connections and forges deep understanding. Ms. McVicker, my cooperating teacher, distributed superhero capes to the boys, each labeled with one of the vowels. This transformed my small intervention group into the Vowel Squad. The Vowel Squad was a big hit with the rest of the class. My performers totally got the vowel sounds. Their peers not only grasped a deep understanding of this topic, but they also developed a new respect for these guys in the Vowel Squad.

Image 47.1

Kids learn how to master a tool like iMovie intuitively. They go from filming and editing to exploring the subtleties of production. If your students don't have iPads, they can use their smartphones to record. If they don't have phones, then it's time for a live performance.

Take a QR code journey through Image 47.1 to access *Hacking Engagement* Episode 7 for an in-depth discussion with Sara Sawdey about the Vowel Squad.

WHAT YOU CAN DO TOMORROW

- **Construct a small cadre of students to peer-teach a challenging topic.** Sara deputized kids she feared would struggle with understanding a complex topic. It's a solid idea to select kids who love to move.

- **Instruct this small group to create an instructional video.** Give the students parameters for your expectations. Sometimes kids focus too much on making videos funny. While humor is great, students have to remember they have a lesson to teach.

- **Teach self-evaluation.** Sara did a great job of debriefing her production team. She was pleased when they cited many ways they could've improved their video. In *Hacking Assessment*, renowned no-grades

> guru Starr Sackstein explores reflection and provides excellent strate-
> gies for turning students into marvelous self-evaluators.
>
> - **Display the video to the remainder of the class.** Debrief the class as
>   well. Find out what they liked and what they didn't. See if the produc-
>   tion team can answer any questions that arise about content.

Some kids just need to move. Exploit this disposition. Deputize these students to create a peer-teaching video.

HACK 48

BANISH BLOGGING BLANDNESS

THE PROBLEM: SOME STUDENTS HATE JOURNALING

I LOVE TO WRITE. It doesn't seem like work. In fact, time simply evaporates when I write. I simply must get ideas out of my head and onto the screen. Writing is remarkably therapeutic for me. But when I was a student and teachers would order me to journal, I'd instantly go into shutdown mode. I'd constrict my body language, frown, and think, *Nyet!* It's odd that someone like me who now enjoys writing once considered journaling the academic equivalent to fingernails scratching the chalkboard.

Ironically, I now require my students to journal. Isn't becoming a teacher humbling? Journaling became a lot cooler with the introduction of the student blog. Sloppy handwriting in a notebook has been replaced by attractive themes, fonts, the ability to add images, media, and links. However, just because the blog format is cool doesn't mean students will automatically love it. Please understand, not all blog prompts inspire. This hack will demonstrate how to craft prompts that even the sixteen-year-old Jim Sturtevant would have embraced.

THE HACK: BRING OUT THE BEST IN STUDENT BLOGGERS

Many researchers promote the idea that real world application—relevance—is a necessity for engagement. Teachers can make writing relevant with blog prompts that inspire students to create experiences for themselves. Ask students to get involved with an experience, such as drawing, building, eating, smelling, climbing, photographing, watching, recording, and analyzing. Then write about what happened. The more intense the experience, the more vivid the student posts.

> **Through this process, they may just find a voice and the experience to express it in diverse ways.**

Edublogs is a platform you can use to introduce students to twenty-first-century journaling. Kidblog is another easy-to-use blogging platform, designed by educators for education. Both allow kids to easily include links, video, audio, and images. These diverse forms of expression are precisely what make blogging so engaging. Many students aren't interested in emulating Laura Ingalls from *Little House on the Prairie* by writing long entries in a personal diary. Blogging liberates student expression. Challenge students to express themselves in different ways:

- photo essays

- video documentaries

- podcasts

- art exhibits

- traditional journal entries

Through this process, they may just find a voice and the experience to express it in diverse ways.

The other amazing aspect of blogging is its collaborative potential. Blogging is public journaling. Once a post is created, classmates, and if you so choose, the entire world, has access. I had a colleague who loved the idea of blogging, but she felt com-

Image 48.1

pelled to read and comment on each student post. She had five classes of bloggers. She was overwhelmed and stalemated. Her solution was peer review. Break students into small blogging circles of four. They can take turns reading and commenting on one another's blogs. The teacher can skim all the posts and comment here and there. Don't let logistics prevent this engaging and important form of student expression.

WHAT YOU CAN DO TOMORROW

- **Prepare a wonderful meal.** Do this today in preparation for tomorrow. It could be as simple as making a peanut butter and jelly sandwich, or it could be a five-star food extravaganza. Capture images of the prep, consumption, and clean-up phase. Everyone can relate to the eating experience, so it will be a great blog post example. The QR code in image 48.1 leads to my prompt for my World Civilization students about the creation of a Buddhist meal.

- **Sign up for Edublogs, Kidblog, or your own preferred blog host.** Most platforms offer a free version. If you pay the nominal subscription fee, however, you and your students will gain access to beautiful themes and other features that teachers may desire. Making blogs visually appealing is engaging in itself. My principal supported my student blogging effort by paying the subscription fee (*Hack within the Hack:* ask your admin to pay small subscription fees that enhance student engagement). Becoming comfortable with the sign-up process will be helpful when you have to guide students through creating their blogs.

- **Create your first blog post.** This should be about your wonderful meal. Be sure to include compelling images and perhaps a paragraph or two. You could include details about why you chose this meal, how you prepared it, and how it tasted.

- **Direct students to comment.** Provide kids with a link to the post. Direct them to read it and look at your images. Encourage them to leave a comment. Get students comfortable with commenting. Commenting on classmates' blogs is an essential part of this experience.

- **Create your first blog prompt.** Tomorrow will be too early to assign it to students, but you want to have it ready to roll. The prompt should pertain to your unit topic, but make certain to challenge kids to do something then reflect on the experience.

Blogging is a magnificent way for students to express themselves. You can make drab journaling ultra-engaging by having students focus on experiential content matter.

HACK 49

TURN YOUR STUDENTS INTO FIVE-YEAR-OLDS

THE PROBLEM: IT'S HARD TO SET CREATIVITY FREE

WHEN YOU WERE five years old and your mom wanted a little break from the responsibility of raising you, she'd give you some paper and crayons, and for the next thirty minutes you would blissfully and silently enter the engagement zone. Across the top of the paper, you'd draw a blue band, which represented the sky. A green band at the bottom was grass. The vast white void between got filled with your house, your dog, a tree, the sun, and a smiling stick figure you. In all honesty, from an artistic standpoint your drawing sucked, but you didn't care. You were totally immersed in what you were doing. When you presented it to her, your mom probably marveled at your masterpiece, but you would have been just fine without all her praise. The truth is, you loved the creative process.

Alas, once you went to kindergarten your artistic innocence was shattered. Your peers and you started to compare artwork. Unlike your mom, your teacher was not as effusive with her praise. You became more interested in the way your art looked in comparison to others and far less content to just create in quiet bliss. For many young people, any fondness for drawing officially ended the day a peer gave your art a miserable review.

THE HACK: LET THEM DRAW

Now that you're a teacher, try promoting drawing in class. Students often groan, "I can't even draw a straight line." In fairness, no one can draw a straight line—that's the function of a ruler. But don't let those crabby statements dissuade you. Kids still

Image 49.1

love to draw. Lay the drawing prompt on them, play a little soothing music in the background, and observe. Just be cool. They'll fuss and fume for a few minutes, then they'll be transported back to the kitchen tables of their tender years. Rowdy classes can become quiet and focused. The period just evaporates when kids draw. Kids look up and can't believe it's time to leave. This is the very definition of engagement.

A few years ago, my students and I made a three-minute video that demonstrates lost innocence in terms of creativity. You can locate the video through the QR code in Image 49.1.

WHAT YOU CAN DO TOMORROW

- **Create a drawing prompt based on your current lesson.** This could be an editorial cartoon, how they think a fictitious figure looks, a new invention, an alien life form, or maybe something as abstract as drawing an emotion like anger.

- **Gather material.** Get plenty of sheets of copy paper and perhaps some straight edges. Allow them to get new paper when they screw up.

- **Set the mood.** Play inspiring music. Allow some kids you trust to play some of their tunes.

- **Work the room.** When students draw, it's an awesome time to mingle and build connections with them. Ask them about their creations, about their lives. Be supportive of their artistic efforts regardless of how awful they might be.

- **Celebrate their creations.** Post their masterpieces in the hallway and encourage students to describe what they drew.

Challenge your students to draw in tomorrow's lesson. After some predictable pushback, you'll be amazed at how engaged they'll be in this creative process.

CHANNEL YOUR INNER YOGA TEACHER

THE PROBLEM: TEACHERS GET BUSY AND FORGET TO BE EMPATHETIC

ONE HECTIC DAY, I had to respond to an email, correct a kid's grade, submit my attendance from the previous period, which I'd forgotten to do, find an assignment prompt for a student who was going home ill and needed it right now, and return a pair of scissors to a colleague all in the thirty seconds before the bell rang. To top it all off, I was in desperate need of a visit to the men's room. Of course, a student needed my attention at that moment. Unfortunately, I didn't give that child my full attention. Even though it happened a long time ago, I still think about the despondent look on her face.

THE HACK: USE COMPASSION TO BUILD
RELATIONSHIPS AND FOSTER ENGAGEMENT

I know some readers are probably muttering *I don't have an inner yoga teacher.* But please consider Amanda Reynolds' words before giving up on this hack. She's an amazing yoga instructor. I know because I've taken many of her classes. She's compassionate, gentle, and encouraging. She inspires stiff students to open. If you interact with Amanda outside of the studio, however, you'll be struck by her intense Ayurvedic pitta nature. She's enthusiastic, active, focused, and competitive. She kids me that I'm a pitta too. *Guilty.* Amanda's story is relevant because her daytime job is to teach high school English. She uses her yoga background to channel—and at times mask—her intensity, build relationships, and engage students.

I asked Amanda straight up about how being a yoga teacher influenced her interactions with high schoolers.

> Oh wow. It's all about compassion. I try to look at a kid, and instead of being stuck in my own brain and thinking about what I have to do next and what this student needs to do next, I take a deep breath and wonder *What's this young person feeling today? What are they going through? Maybe this person needs me to slow down and be more gentle, or maybe I need to change my tone. What am I sensing?* And then, I realize that before I do or say anything else, I need to ask a simple question: *How are you doing today?*

Amanda uses intuition and friendly, solicitous conversation to forge solid student-teacher bonds. Such relationships are essential to engagement. The relationships Amanda has encouraged have transformed her class because students feel respected enough to play a crucial curriculum-planning role. Amanda constantly asks herself, *Would I want to do this assignment?* She then asks her students whether they're interested in it. One day she learned they didn't want to read *All Quiet on the Western Front,* so she didn't assign it. Instead, she gave students freedom to choose their own paths to study the horrors of war. She didn't limit them to World War I or reading a very old novel, but instead gave them decision-making authority. As you probably guessed, engagement blossomed.

WHAT YOU CAN DO TOMORROW

- **Engage your intuition.** Think of a student who's struggling. Create an excuse to interact with this child one-on-one. Don't discuss school. During the conversation, engage your senses and your intuition and see if you can learn anything about why this youngster is having a hard time.

- **Ask: "How are you doing?"** Many people greet you with, "What's up?" or, "How are you doing?" with zero expectation that you'll actually tell them. When you ask this question, be certain to stay present and engaged for the answer.

- **Ask your students a courageous question.** If you ask kids whether they want to do an assignment, some will probably say no. That's fine: Challenge them to offer alternatives. You may or may not use their suggestions, but you'll certainly gain valuable insight.

Strive to interact with students compassionately and to gain valuable insight into them and how you can make your class more engaging.

CONCLUSION

GOOD LUCK

BLEAK NEWS GREETED me in the summer of 2010. I was five years from retirement. While I had always enjoyed teaching, part of me was ready to commence a new chapter in my life. Thirty years is a long time to do anything. But thirty years doesn't come close to representing the average American life span. I've never permitted my job to define me, so I was looking forward to spending the next five years planning my next professional excursion.

On our teacher workday that fateful August, the day before the students arrived, I learned that the State of Ohio's Public Employee Retirement Systems had been devastated by the Recession of 2008. The upshot was my October 2015 retirement target would be undermined. I'm a positive person, but it was like being informed in the last few miles of a marathon that the race would be extended.

The next twenty-four hours were painful. I felt like I'd fulfilled my part of the obligation to the good people of Ohio. I like having a plan, and this development really shook me. As has happened frequently in my career when I've been confronted by significant personal challenges, all those feelings of turmoil evaporated at 7:30 a.m. the next day—the first day of school. A sweet fourteen-year-old girl marched up to me, smiled, and raised

> **It suddenly dawned on me how selfish I'd been. I remembered what an awesome privilege it is to help kids blossom.**

her right hand. I looked at her quizzically, but then I instinctively raised my right hand too. Then I caught on and we high-fived one another. She said, "I'm so glad you're my teacher. I've heard awesome things about you."

I thanked her and then quickly shuffled down the hall to the small men's room in the faculty lounge. I shut the door, locked it, rotated to a corner, and broke into passionate sobs. It was so intense, so unexpected. It suddenly dawned on me how selfish I'd been. I remembered what an awesome privilege it is to help kids blossom.

I composed myself, blew my nose, stared at myself in the mirror, and thought *If you're going to be a teacher for the foreseeable future, be a great one.*

In August of 2016 I'll begin my thirty-second year of bonding, encouraging, and learning from youngsters. And there's no end in sight. I'm grateful for my experience in 2010. It shamed and inspired me. Since then, I've become a much better teacher. I'm the old guy in the building who's not afraid to try things. I've recommitted myself to compassionate teaching. I love learning new tactics from younger tech-savvy colleagues. As a result, my students have thrived.

The past five years in the classroom have been magical. I published my first book. I've made amazing friends with podcasts and on Voxer. And now, I'm so excited to offer this book, which wouldn't have been possible if it weren't for a sweet and tender compliment offered by a child on a late summer morning. Maybe I can be that motivating force for you.

This book is stocked with ideas that can transform your class. If you had the commitment and fortitude to purchase and then read these pages, your heart is in exactly the right place. This disposition is the most important part. The rest is just trial and error. Take the hacks in this book and give them a shot. Who knows? The next five years could be magical for you.

Good luck with engaging your students.

PREVIEW
JAMES ALAN STURTEVANT'S
HACKING ENGAGEMENT AGAIN

HACK

CONTEXTUALIZE...
CONTEXTUALIZE...
CONTEXTUALIZE

THE PROBLEM: CHRONOLOGICAL IGNORANCE
IS THE ENEMY OF ENGAGEMENT

I TEACH HISTORY. EVEN as a boy, I was a history nerd. Recently, I was enjoying the company of friends at a party. My buddies all have college degrees and are successful in their chosen professions. A historical topic surfaced. I decided to conduct a little wine-inspired experiment. I just listened to them pontificate about a subject I knew a lot about. This is generally not my disposition when vino veritas is factored in. What took place was fascinating. While my friends had a working understanding of the topic, their background chronology was out of whack, which, of course, did a serious number on their understanding.

If intelligent adults struggle with context on what would seem common historical knowledge, it would be foolhardy to assume that K-12 students, aside from the budding history nerds, would have a clue about the order of events. Contextual ignorance does not just apply to events, but also processes. Students in math, science, and language arts must understand many processes like the quadratic equation, the scientific method, and MLA citation. Chronological awareness with such concepts breeds confidence, which is crucial to engagement. Let's inspire some of that awareness with a cool virtual timeline builder.

THE HACK: CHALLENGE KIDS TO
BUILD A VIRTUAL CHRONOLOGY

ReadWriteThink is a neat website populated by helpful education tools. For this hack, we'll use their online timeline creator. Please follow the QR code in Image 51.1 to access this virtual tool.

Image 51.1

When one thinks of timelines, one typically thinks of historical chronologies. However, the same ordering could be applied to the six steps of the scientific method. The building of this virtual timeline could be a foundational experience for students. Being able to contextualize the steps in a process, or the order of events, fosters academic confidence and opens the door to engagement.

Last semester, my World Civ class was embarking on a unit addressing 20th century Chinese history. My kids knew virtually nothing about this important topic. I decided the first step in this academic journey would be for my kids to create virtual timelines. Here's the prompt I gave students, which can easily be altered to match concepts or processes in other subjects:

- I gave them a starting point (the Boxer Rebellion 1899) and an ending point (the Communist Victory 1949).

- I challenged them to plot seven important events in between.

- I required that each event include a title, the year it took place, an explanation as to why the event was important, and a public domain or creative commons image. (Imagine some of the cool imagery students could find for quadratic equations and the scientific method!)

Once your students complete their timelines, direct them to select the finish button. This is a crucial step on ReadWriteThink. If kids don't hit finish, they may lose what they've created. Once they select finish, they can download a PDF and share it with their classmates and you. See examples in Images 51.2 and 51.3.

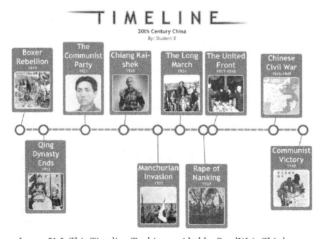

Image 51.2: This Timeline Tool is provided by ReadWriteThink.org, a website developed by the National Council of Teachers of English.

Image 51.3: This Timeline Tool is provided by ReadWriteThink.org, a
website developed by the National Council of Teachers of English.

The next day, the teacher can formulate small groups so students can compare time-lines. There'll be lively discussion about event choices, image choices, and explaining to one another why they found certain events, or junctures in a process, important.

Kids are honest. Instructors can learn a lot from unsolicited feedback. Many students commented about how much the creation of this timeline helped them prepare for the topic. Prompting students to contextualize is powerful.

WHAT YOU CAN DO TOMORROW

- **Create your own timeline on ReadWriteThink.** This will familiarize you with the process. Select finish, and download the image as a PDF.

- **Select an important topic.** This would be a great introduction for a unit. It could also be used effectively for describing the steps in a process.

- **Formulate small discussion groups.** After the timelines are created, students should compare and contrast their timelines with classmates. This will further help kids contextualize because peers may have included events they didn't consider.

When students are able to place events or processes in context, they become confident and engaged academic explorers.

HACK

RECRUIT STUDENTS TO EMBARK ON AN ACADEMIC HERO'S JOURNEY

THE PROBLEM: STUDENTS RARELY CELEBRATE, MUCH LESS ACKNOWLEDGE, THEIR ACADEMIC ACCOMPLISHMENTS

IT WAS MY first day as a third-grade student. Our teacher was calling each of us to her desk to turn in the reams of paperwork that schools used to require on day one. As I waited my turn, I leafed through my new textbook, pausing on the pictures. I navigated toward the end of the book, and the final math section startled me. The pages were populated with very advanced-looking equations. They seemed like the scribblings of a mad scientist on his chalkboard. I wondered, *Wow. That looks complicated. I don't know if I'll be able to do these problems.* Nine months later, school was about to dismiss for summer. Remarkably, we were breezing through the unit with the equations that looked so intimidating. I vividly remember thinking, *I thought these problems were going to be hard, but they're easy. I need to remember this next year.* I give the young me a lot of credit for this mental vote of confidence.

THE HACK: INSPIRE FUTURE CONFIDENCE BY CHALLENGING STUDENTS TO CHRONICLE A PAST ACHIEVEMENT

Lisa Highfill, Kelly Hilton, and Sarah Landis are the co-creators of HyperDocs. These ladies have designed a remarkable website that provides teachers with digital lesson templates and plenty of sample HyperDocs. Aside from their outstanding organization, the templates are beautiful, which should never be underestimated. To begin creating, simply FILE>MAKE A COPY and complete the stages of the lesson cycle by adding instructions and resources. The HyperDoc Girls have a template for the Hero's Journey. Their template contains five stages:

Phase 1: The Call to Adventure
Phase 2: Entering the Unknown
Phase 3: Meeting the Mentor
Phase 4: Transformation
Phase 5: Mastery

Follow the QR code in Image 52.1 to access the HyperDoc Girls website, and scroll down to reach the Hero's Journey template. This hack will inspire students to recreate an academic hero's journey.

Conduct a brainstorming session. This can be done individually, or in small groups. Prompt kids to list their proudest academic achievements. Under each achievement, students should then record obstacles they had to overcome. Once completed, students need to designate the one challenge they found particularly thorny. This will become their hero's quest.

Image 52.1

Provide students with a link to the Hero's Journey HyperDoc template. Instruct them to make a copy. Challenge kids to research the hero's journey stages. What does each mean? What would make good examples for each stage? The HyperDoc template should act like a storyboard. Students can insert images, text, and links. Once completed, they can then take their storyboard and produce something awesome. They could record a podcast, craft a mural, perform a skit, or create a video.

The final stage of the academic hero's quest will be to create a narrative. This exercise asks students to take what they've learned through recounting a past success and then apply it to the present. Prompt students to formulate a plan on how they can replicate success when complicated challenges arise in your class this semester. Access Image 52.2 to hear my conversation with the HyperDoc Girls.

Image 52.2

WHAT YOU CAN DO TOMORROW

- **Recount a personal story of academic success.** Often, students are convinced their teachers just breezed through school. Tell your students about an academic obstacle you found particularly challenging, and explain how you ultimately prevailed! This will help humanize you and perhaps inspire your kids.

- **Inspire students to designate a personal success for the academic hero's quest.** If students are totally stumped, you may even let them use a non-academic example.

- **Expose kids to the HyperDoc Girls Hero's Journey template.** This wonderful template will be the journey storyboard. They will create their productions from this lesson flow.

- **Guide students toward applying this success to the current semester.** I suggested a narrative, but it could be another format. The key is for kids to internalize this: *I succeeded before. I can do it again.*

By reliving a past success, students will be more willing to embark on another academic hero's quest.

HACK

TUNE IN THE 21ST CENTURY WALKIE-TALKIE

THE PROBLEM: BOYS AREN'T EXCITED ABOUT READING

WHEN I WAS in third grade, the last thing in the world I wanted to do was read a book. What was true then is still true today for many young boys.

Debbie Olsen, an inclusion teacher from Long Island, New York, certainly recognizes this attitude. So she decided to use Voxer, the 21st century walkie talkie app, to get nine-year-old boys excited about reading. She says, "I began using Voxer for a book club. I would like to tell you that I put a lot of thought and careful planning into this, but that would not be true. My gut instinct was that Voxer could be a "hook" to motivate these readers, so I ran with it."

I was instantly drawn to Debbie's idea! My first reaction when I started playing with Voxer was, *This is a lot like the walkie-talkie set I got on my tenth birthday.* I loved that toy! My posse and I played with them constantly in my little neighborhood. There were only two units that we had to share, and from a performance standpoint, my ancient walkie-talkie sucked! That's not the case with Voxer. Its range is global and its sound quality is solid. The major

Students will be excited about using this tool and the reading will be the vehicle.

issue is inadvertent butt-voxing from a phone in a back pocket. I once transmitted a fifteen-minute dead air vox to my teacher group. Fortunately, I didn't say or do anything too stupid during that marathon!

THE HACK: CREATE A VOXER BOOK CLUB

Here's how Debbie created her Voxer book club: "I sent a letter home to their parents asking them to download the free Voxer app. I told the boys about a special project we were going to try."

She continues, "I then demonstrated how Voxer works. I had asked a colleague from another school to be ready to vox with me. My class watched in amazement as I chatted back and forth with my remote friend. We even used some CB lingo, *Breaker, breaker. What's your 20?* The boys literally went nuts! The goal was to make it fun and get them voxing first before I tried to get them voxing about the book. The first night, the boys voxed a million times. I listened but did not respond. There were some ridiculous voxes with sounds and general boy silliness. The next day, we discussed how fun it was to use Voxer, but also about being respectful."

First, Debbie got her kids hooked on Voxer, and then she hooked them on the book. "I then gave out the books and told the boys it was theirs to keep. They loved that! We planned how much reading they thought they would be able to do for the

Image 53.1

day (both in and out of school). I did not say that they had to vox each day. I let that happen naturally. Every one of them had multiple voxes each evening." Follow Image 53.1 to hear Debbie discuss her Voxer-infused lesson plan.

Boy, I wish I could have experienced Debbie's class as a third-grader!

WHAT YOU CAN DO TOMORROW

- **Craft a letter to parents explaining your objectives.** Some parents may object to their child participating in Voxer or downloading the app. Have these students form a separate book club and they can meet and discuss in person.

- **Demonstrate Voxer.** This was a brilliant idea on Debbie's part! A successful demonstration is a great hook.

- **Designate a reading for the full Voxer book club treatment.** Voxer is your hook! Students will be excited about using this tool and the reading will be the vehicle. Choose a reading that will elicit great discussion.

Create a Voxer book club. It's a cool way to hook reluctant readers.

BUY
HACKING ENGAGEMENT AGAIN

AT HACKLEARNINGBOOKS.COM

HACKING EDUCATION
10 Quick Fixes For Every School

By Mark Barnes (@markbarnes19) & Jennifer Gonzalez (@cultofpedagogy)

In the award-winning first Hack Learning Series book, *Hacking Education*, Mark Barnes and Jennifer Gonzalez employ decades of teaching experience and hundreds of discussions with education thought leaders to show you how to find and hone the quick fixes that every school and classroom need. Using a Hacker's mentality, they provide **one Aha moment after another** with 10 Quick Fixes For Every School—solutions to everyday problems and teaching methods that any teacher or administrator can implement immediately.

"Barnes and Gonzalez don't just solve problems; they turn teachers into hackers—a transformation that is right on time."

—Don Wettrick, Author of *Pure Genius*

HACKING PROJECT BASED LEARNING
10 Easy Steps to PBL and Inquiry in the Classroom

By Ross Cooper (@rosscoops31) and Erin Murphy (@murphysmusings5)

As questions and mysteries around PBL and inquiry continue to swirl, experienced classroom teachers and school administrators Ross Cooper and Erin Murphy have written a book that will empower those intimidated by PBL to cry, "I can do this!" while at the same time providing added value for those who are already familiar with the process. Impacting teachers and leaders around the world, *Hacking Project Based Learning* demystifies what PBL is all about with **10 hacks that construct a simple path** that educators and students can easily follow to achieve success. Forget your prior struggles with project based learning. This book makes PBL an amazing gift you can give all students tomorrow!

"*Hacking Project Based Learning* is a classroom essential. Its ten simple 'hacks' will guide you through the process of setting up a learning environment in which students will thrive from start to finish."

—DANIEL H. PINK, *NEW YORK TIMES* BESTSELLING AUTHOR OF *DRIVE*

HACKING ASSESSMENT
10 Ways to Go Gradeless in a Traditional Grades School

By Starr Sackstein (@mssackstein)

In the bestselling *Hacking Assessment,* award-winning teacher and world-renowned formative assessment expert Starr Sackstein unravels one of education's oldest mysteries: How to assess learning without grades—even in a school that uses numbers, letters, GPAs, and report cards. While many educators can only muse about the possibility of a world without grades, teachers like Sackstein are **reimagining education**. In this unique, eagerly-anticipated book, Sackstein shows you exactly how to create a remarkable no-grades classroom like hers, a vibrant place where students grow, share, thrive, and become independent learners who never ask, "What's this worth?"

"The beauty of the book is that it is not an empty argument against grades—but rather filled with valuable alternatives that are practical and will help to refocus the classroom on what matters most."

—ADAM BELLOW, WHITE HOUSE PRESIDENTIAL INNOVATION FELLOW

HACKING LEADERSHIP
10 Ways Great Leaders Inspire Learning That Teachers, Students, and Parents Love

By Joe Sanfelippo (@joe_sanfelippo) and Tony Sinanis (@tonysinanis)

In the runaway bestseller *Hacking Leadership*, internationally-known school leaders Joe Sanfelippo and Tony Sinanis bring readers inside schools that few stakeholders have ever seen—places where students not only come first but have a unique voice in teaching and learning. Sanfelippo and Sinanis ignore the bureaucracy that stifles many leaders, focusing instead on building a culture of **engagement, transparency and, most important, fun**. *Hacking Leadership* has superintendents, principals, and teacher leaders around the world employing strategies they never before believed possible and learning how to lead from the middle. Want to revolutionize teaching and learning at your school or district? *Hacking Leadership* is your blueprint. Read it today, energize teachers and learners tomorrow!

"The authors do a beautiful job of helping leaders focus inward, instead of outward. This is an essential read for leaders who are, or want to lead, learner-centered schools."

—George Couros, Author of *The Innovator's Mindset*

HACKING SCHOOL CULTURE
Designing Compassionate Classrooms

By Angela Stockman (@angelastockman) and Ellen Feig Gray (@ellenfeiggray)

Bullying prevention and character building programs are deepening our awareness of how today's kids struggle and how we might help, but many agree: They aren't enough to create school cultures where students and staff flourish. This inspired Angela Stockman and Ellen Feig Gray to begin seeking out systems and educators who were getting things right. Their experiences taught them that the real game changers are using a human-centered approach. Inspired by other design thinkers, many teachers are creating learning environments where seeking a greater understanding of themselves and others is the highest standard. They're also realizing that compassion is best cultivated in the classroom, not the boardroom or the auditorium. It's here that we learn how to pull one another close. It's here that we begin to negotiate the distances between us, too.

"*Hacking School Culture: Designing Compassionate Classrooms* is a valuable addition to the HACK Learning Series. It provides concrete support and suggestions for teachers to improve their interactions with their students at the same time they enrich their own professional experiences. Although primarily aimed at K-12 classrooms, the authors' insightful suggestions have given me, a veteran college professor, new insights into positive classroom dynamics which I have already begun to incorporate into my classes."

—LOUISE HAINLINE, PH.D., PROFESSOR OF PSYCHOLOGY, BROOKLYN COLLEGE OF CUNY

HACKING EARLY LEARNING
10 Building Blocks to Success in Pre-K-3 That All Teachers and School Leaders Should Know

By Jessica Cabeen (@jessicacabeen)

School readiness, closing achievement gaps, partnering with families, and innovative learning are just a few of the reasons the early learning years are the most critical years in a child's life. In what ways have schools lost the critical components of early learning — preschool through third grade — and how can we intentionally bring those ideas and instructional strategies back? In *Hacking Early Learning*, Kindergarten school leader, early childhood education specialist, and Minnesota State Principal of the Year Jessica Cabeen provides strategies for teachers, principals, and district administrators for best practices in preschool through third grade, including connecting these strategies to all grade levels.

"Jessica Cabeen is not afraid to say she's learned from her mistakes and misconceptions. But it is those mistakes and misconceptions that qualify her to write this book, with its wonderfully user-friendly format. For each problem specified, there is a hack and actionable advice presented as "What You Can Do Tomorrow" and "A Blueprint for Full Implementation." Jessica's leadership is informed by both head and heart and, because of that, her wisdom will be of value to those who wish to teach and lead in the early childhood field."

-RAE PICA, EARLY CHILDHOOD EDUCATION KEYNOTE SPEAKER AND AUTHOR OF *WHAT IF EVERYBODY UNDERSTOOD CHILD DEVELOPMENT?*

HACKING ENGAGEMENT
50 Tips & Tools to Engage Teachers and Learners Daily

By James Alan Sturtevant (@jamessturtevant)

Some students hate your class. Others are just bored. Many are too nice, or too afraid, to say anything about it. Don't let it bother you; it happens to the best of us. But now, it's **time to engage!** In *Hacking Engagement*, the seventh book in the *Hack Learning Series*, veteran high school teacher, author, and popular podcaster James Sturtevant provides 50—that's right five-oh— tips and tools that will engage even the most reluctant learners daily. Sold in dozens of countries around the world, *Hacking Engagement* has become educator's go-to guide for better student engagement in all grades and subjects. In fact, this book is so popular, Sturtevant penned a follow-up, *Hacking Engagement Again*, which brings 50 more powerful strategies. Find both at HackLearningBooks.com.

HACKING DIGITAL LEARNING STRATEGIES
10 Ways to Launch EdTech Missions in Your Classroom

By Shelly Sanchez Terrell (@ShellTerrell)

In this breakthrough book, international EdTech presenter and NAPW Woman of the Year Shelly Sanchez Terrell demonstrates the power of EdTech Missions—lessons and projects that inspire learners to use web tools and social media to innovate, research, collaborate, problem-solve, campaign, crowd fund, crowdsource, and publish. The 10 Missions in *Hacking DLS* are more than enough to transform how teachers integrate technology, but there's also much more here.

Included in the book is a **38-page Mission Toolkit**, complete with reproducible mission cards, badges, polls, and other handouts that you can copy and distribute to students immediately.

"The secret to Shelly's success as an education collaborator on a global scale is that she shares information most revered by all educators, information that is original, relevant, and vetted, combining technology with proven education methodology in the classroom. This book provides relevance to a 21st century educator."

—THOMAS WHITBY, AUTHOR, PODCASTER, BLOGGER, CONSULTANT, CO-FOUNDER OF #EDCHAT

HACKING CLASSROOM MANAGEMENT
10 Ideas To Help You Become the Type of Teacher They Make Movies About

By Mike Roberts (@baldroberts)

Utah English Teacher of the Year and sought-after speaker Mike Roberts brings you 10 quick and easy classroom management hacks that will make your classroom the place to be for all your students. He shows you how to create an amazing learning environment that actually makes discipline, rules, and consequences obsolete, no matter if you're a new teacher or a 30-year veteran teacher.

"Mike writes from experience; he's learned, sometimes the hard way, what works and what doesn't, and he shares those lessons in this fine little book. The book is loaded with specific, easy-to-apply suggestions that will help any teacher create and maintain a classroom where students treat one another with respect, and where they learn."

—CHRIS CROWE, ENGLISH PROFESSOR AT BYU, PAST PRESIDENT OF ALAN, AUTHOR OF *DEATH COMING UP THE HILL*, *GETTING AWAY WITH MURDER: THE TRUE STORY OF THE EMMETT TILL CASE; MISSISSIPPI TRIAL, 1955*

HACKING THE WRITING WORKSHOP
Redesign with Making in Mind

By Angela Stockman (@AngelaStockman)

Agility matters. This is what Angela Stockman learned when she left the classroom over a decade ago to begin supporting young writers and their teachers in schools. What she learned transformed her practice and led to the publication of her primer on this topic: *Make Writing: 5 Teaching Strategies that Turn Writer's Workshop Into a Maker Space*. Now, Angela is back with more stories from the road and plenty of new thinking to share. In *Make Writing*, Stockman upended the traditional writing workshop by combining it with the popular ideas that drive the maker space. Now, she is expanding her concepts and strategies and breaking new ground in *Hacking the Writing Workshop*.

"Good writing is good thinking. This is a book about how to think better, for yourself and with others."

—DAVE GRAY, FOUNDER OF XPLANE, AND AUTHOR OF *THE CONNECTED COMPANY*, *GAMESTORMING*, AND *LIMINAL THINKING*

by Teachonomy

THE UNSERIES
Teaching Reimagined

The uNseries is for teachers who love the uNlovable, accept the uNacceptable, rebuild the broken, and help the genius soar. Through each book in the uNseries you will learn how to continue your growth as a teacher, leader, and influencer. The goal is that together we can become better than we ever could have alone. Each chapter uNveils an important principle to ponder, uNravels a plan that you can put into place to make an even greater impact, and uNleashes an action step for you to take to be a better educator. Learn more about the **uNseries and everything uN** at unseriesbooks.com.

RESOURCES FROM TIMES 10

SITES:
times10books.com
hacklearning.org
hacklearningbooks.com
unseriesbooks.com
teachonomy.com

PODCASTS:
hacklearningpodcast.com
jamesalansturtevant.com/podcast
teachonomy.com/podcast

FREE TOOLKIT FOR TEACHERS:
hacklearningtoolkit.com

ON TWITTER:

@HackMyLearning
#HackLearning
#HackLearningDaily
#WeTeachuN
#HackingLeadership
#HackingMath
#HackingLiteracy
#HackingEngagement
#HackingHomework

#HackingPBL
#MakeWriting
#EdTechMissions
#MovieTeacher
#HackingEarlyLearning
#CompassionateClassrooms
#HackGoogleEdu
#ParentMantras

HACK LEARNING ON FACEBOOK:
facebook.com/hacklearningseries

HACK LEARNING ON INSTAGRAM:
hackmylearning

ABOUT THE AUTHOR

 **James Alan Sturtevant** has taught in Delaware County, in Central Ohio, for over three decades. His first book, *You've Gotta Connect* details how teachers can build essential relationships with students. He has appeared on many popular podcasts and authored guest posts on Edutopia, the Huffington Post, and Principal Leadership. Sturtevant remains committed to helping teachers forge strong relationships with kids, but his true passion is student engagement. With his new book and podcast, *Hacking Engagement*, he helps educators create classrooms and schools that captivate kids and empower them to learn.

ACKNOWLEDGEMENTS

I WOULD LIKE TO thank my friend and publisher Mark Barnes. This book was conceptualized and then created as a result of our many casual and thoroughly enjoyable conversations. I'd like to thank my friend and editor Ruth Arseneault. Ruth is a wordsmith extraordinaire. I'd like to acknowledge all of my amazing educational comrades who enriched the pages of *Hacking Engagement* with their brilliance. And finally, I owe my largest debt of gratitude to my clan. Thank you Jason, Niki, David, Maria, little Kaia, and Penny, my life partner and biggest supporter.

PUBLICATIONS

Times 10 is helping all education stakeholders improve every aspect of teaching and learning. We are committed to solving big problems with simple ideas. We bring you content from experts, shared through multiple channels, including books, podcasts, and an array of social networks. Our mantra is simple: Read it today; fix it tomorrow.

Stay in touch with us at #HackLearning on Twitter and on the Hack Learning Facebook page. To work with our authors and consultants, visit our Team page at hacklearning.org.

Made in the USA
Monee, IL
28 September 2020